OXFORD INTENSIVE ENGLISH COURSES

D1824956

FAST FORWARD

Advanced

CLASSBOOK

LAURETTE LONG

Oxford University Press

Oxford University Press, Walton Street, Oxford OX2 6DP

Oxford   New York   Toronto   Madrid
Kuala Lumpur   Singapore   Hong Kong   Tokyo
Delhi   Bombay   Madras   Calcutta   Karachi
Nairobi   Dar es Salaam   Cape Town
Melbourne   Auckland

and associated companies in
Berlin   Ibadan

Oxford and *Oxford English* are trade
marks of Oxford University Press

ISBN 0 19 432312 9

Set by Pentacor PLC

Printed in Hong Kong

Contents

INTRODUCTORY UNIT   7

UNIT 1
Who's Who?   10

UNIT 2
Testing Testing   17

UNIT 3
'Mirror, Mirror . . .'   24

UNIT 4
Stereotypes   32

UNIT 5
Clothes Power   40

UNIT 6
Advertising   48

UNIT 7
The Right Stuff   55

UNIT 8
Success   65

OPTIONAL ACTIVITIES   80

SOLUTIONS   86

The author and publishers would like to thank all the copyright holders for their permission to reproduce the extracts in this book.

Adventures in the Image Trade (p.26), the extract from *Fearlessness* by David T Lykken (p.51) and *Tips For Speakers* (p.63) permission from Psychology Today Magazine ©1982, American Psychological Association. Advertisement for BP (p.30) © BP Oil Ltd., 1984. *Much More Than A Pretty Face* (p.36) by Liz Forgan. *Dressing the Truth* (p.42) from the Sunday Times Magazine 8.3.87 © Times Newspapers Ltd. *Cosmo's Top Ten Ads* (p.53) Cosmopolitan (UK Edition). *A Lark in the Arc* and *Paris by Air* (pp.56 & 57) from Newsweek 11.2.81 and © 1981 Newsweek, Inc. all rights reserved. Reprinted by permission. Extract from *Brain Games* (p.80) by Richard B Fisher published by Fontana 1981. *The Three-Bottle Problem* (p.83) from *The Five-Day Course In Thinking* (p.83) by Edward de Bono (Allen Lane The Penguin Press, 1968) © Edward de Bono 1967.

The publishers have been unable to trace the copyright holders of: the extract and diagrams from *Know Your Own Personality* H Eysenck and G Wilson (pp. 11, 12, 15, 16, & 86); *Contrary Imaginations* (p.20) by Liam Hudson; *Quibble's Glasses* and *Steak Strategy* (p.23) and would be pleased to hear from them. They would also be pleased to hear from any other parties who feel they hold rights to any of the texts included.

The publisher would also like to thank the following for their permission to reproduce photographs:
Aquarius
Bridgeman Art Library
British Shoe Corporation
Charles of the Ritz
Frank Spooner Pictures
Robert Harding Picture Library
The Image Bank
Intercity Central Advertising Services
Iain McKnell
Popperfoto
Rex Features
Young and Rubicam Ltd/Andreas Heumann
BSB Dorland

Illustrations by
Mel Calman
Stefan Chabluk
Robert Duncan
Martin Salisbury
Oxford Illustrators
Gray Joliffe

PREFACE

Twenty-seven years ago I bounded into my first classroom full of idealism and revolutionary fervour, ready to transform the British education system at a stroke. One year later, I crawled out of the same classroom and headed for the USA, vowing that I would earn my living doing *anything* except teach.

My initial acknowledgements must therefore go to the teachers and students of Gordon School in Providence, Rhode Island, who persuaded me to change my mind, transformed my attitudes to teaching and education, and made me realize what a delight the whole thing can be. They were even cunning enough to get me tied up in countless activities outside school where I had the great good fortune to meet yet more stimulating 'fringe' teachers and educators, and to learn that there are no fixed times and places for teaching and learning, and no fixed roles either. Heartfelt thanks, therefore, to all those others, in particular Elaine Ostroff and Elizabeth Ginsburg and members of The Looking Glass Theatre for children. Returning to England in the 1970s I had yet another stroke of luck. Abandoning secondary education for primary, I was thrown into the midst of the classroom revolution taking place in primary schools in Leicestershire and Cambridgeshire, and again came into contact with those unsung heroes of the education system, the ordinary teachers whose names will probably never be famous but who continue year after year to inspire their students and their colleagues by their enthusiasm, commitment and imagination. Since starting out in EFL, my thanks go to many people. First, all my teachers for the RSA course in Cambridge, in particular Rod Bolitho, Jennifer Day, Chris George, and Mario Rinvolucri who have helped so many others. In France, the organizers of The English Teachers' Meetings in Toulouse deserve a special mention, in particular Jeremy Mell and Mike O'Donoghue, who later became my colleagues and with whom I was thus able to continue discussing the existential 'angoisse' of the EFL teacher on a daily basis over coffee and imported digestive biscuits . Thanks also go to Lilian Buleon at the Ecole Nationale Supérieure des Constructions Aéronautiques and Yves Rengade at the Ecole Nationale de l'Aviation Civile for their encouragement and enthusiasm when I first began this book; Susan Entwhistle and Jeffrey Patten, who greatly contributed to the planning stages; Anne Pechou, who always has something interesting to say about everything, Michele Flood, who shared her office and her views on student autonomy with equal generosity; and finally the members of the English Department at the Ecole Nationale de l'Aviation Civile in Toulouse, who just make going to work so nice.

Friends and family can always be relied upon for support and encouragement. Devotion exceeded the realms of duty however when they graciously agreed to be roped in for the recordings and exhibited not only patience but unsuspected depths of talent. Warmest thanks therefore to my parents, Marjorie and Lawrence Binns, and cousins and friends Stephanie and Chris Bouckley, Joanna Franklin, Tracy Johnson, Kaye Kneen, Tim O'Shea, David Pearl, and Annie Wharton. I am particularly grateful to my husband, Mike Long, not so much for all the recording and editing he did, but more for his amazing range of anti-depressant gourmet dinners. Thanks are also due to Shelagh Rixon who gave invaluable help with the cassette, and cast a keen eye over the manuscript.

During several years working with active and innovative colleagues it's impossible to remember just where many ideas started to grow. I do know that the work of Stephen Krashen has had a strong influence on my development as an EFL teacher; and in a more indirect way, Gertrude Moskowitz, whose ideas have become part of the air breathed in by countless EFL teachers. Apologies to anyone whose ideas have unconsciously influenced the contents of this course, and who has not received an acknowledgement. Last, but perhaps first, thank you, wherever you are, to those students from ENSICA and ENAC, from LANCO, from Airbus Industrie, from CNES, who not only provided hours of good fun in the classroom, but also shaped this book.

Laurette Long

Introductions

1   Divide into groups of three or four and complete the following information sheet together. When you have finished, choose a spokesperson to introduce the group to the rest of the class.

Group Information Sheet

Names (in alphabetical order) _____

Nationalities _____

Jobs/Principal Occupations _____

Languages spoken in group _____

Previous experience of studying English (where? when? how long?)_____
_____

Which (English) language areas do you feel are your strongest? _____
(e.g. writing, listening, speaking, vocabulary, grammar, etc.)
_____

Which areas of English would you most like to improve? _____
(e.g. writing, oral comprehension, fluency in speaking, vocabulary, etc.)
_____

What are your main reasons for coming on this course, other than to improve your English? _____
(e.g. to help you in your work, for pleasure, etc.)
_____

2 Working with a new group, discuss the following points, giving reasons for your opinions or examples from your own experience. Use a 'circulating secretary', i.e. student 1 make notes on question 1, student 2 make notes on question 2, etc. If you feel the questions are not clear, or need qualifying, you can re-phrase them.

1 What do you think are the most effective ways of learning English inside the classroom?

2 Do you consider that language learning only takes place within the classroom?

3 When learning a language in the classroom:
   a in what ways do you think the teacher can be most useful or helpful?
   b in what ways do you think you can best help yourself?

4 How would you rate the following factors in language learning?

	IMPORTANT	NOT IMPORTANT
1 A 'good ear' for languages	☐	☐
2 High intelligence	☐	☐
3 High motivation	☐	☐
4 Understanding what is being said	☐	☐
5 Having mistakes corrected	☐	☐
6 A relaxed, stress-free environment	☐	☐
7 Using the foreign language to help you to do other things, e.g. solve problems, complete tasks, get information, etc.	☐	☐
8 The student's personality	☐	☐
9 Developing learning strategies (e.g. keeping records of new vocabulary, using monolingual dictionaries, listening to the news in the foreign language every day, etc,)	☐	☐
10 Other (please specify)		

Secretaries report back to the class. Is there general agreement? Or do people hold widely varying opinions about language learning?

3

1 In pairs, look at the list of words below. Put them in the diagram according to whether you think they describe 'a good student', 'a good teacher' or both.

intelligent   well-trained
experienced   organized
outgoing   motivated

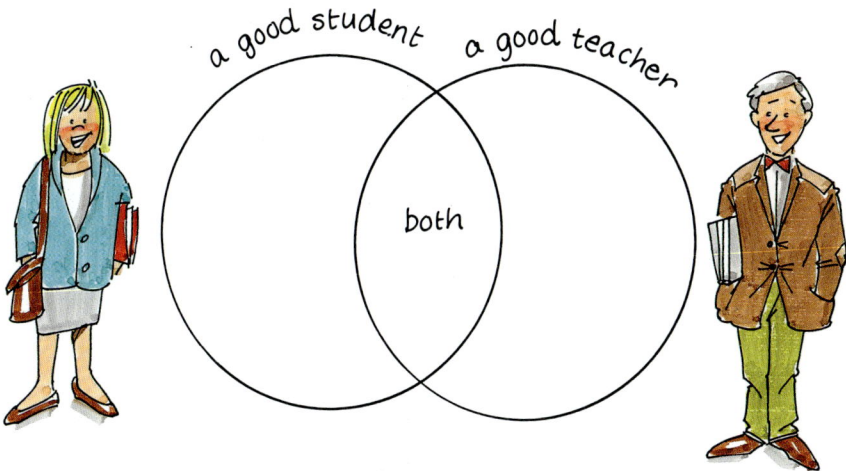

What do *you* think makes 'a good student' or 'a good teacher'? Note your ideas and add any words or phrases to the diagram.

2 ⌨ Listen to find out how many of the words you put on the diagram were used by the speakers. How did their ideas compare with yours?
Discuss with the rest of the class. Is there anything new that you want to add to the ideas that came out of the questionnaire on page 8?

UNIT 1   WHO'S WHO?

1

Look at the cartoon below. Who are the two people in it, and how might one of them be able to help the other?

2

1 Work on the following tasks in groups of three or four.

1 'Psy' words, e.g. psyche, psychologist . . . can you think of any other words beginning with 'psy'?
2 How do you pronounce 'psyche' in English? Which letter is silent?
3 Do you know which language 'psyche' comes from? Do you know what it means in that language?
4 Psychiatrists and psychologists both study human behaviour and the workings of the human mind. In what way are they different? Discuss your ideas with the rest of the class. You'll find out more about this as you listen.

2 While listening, try to complete the diagram below to show the differences and similarities between psychologists and psychiatrists.

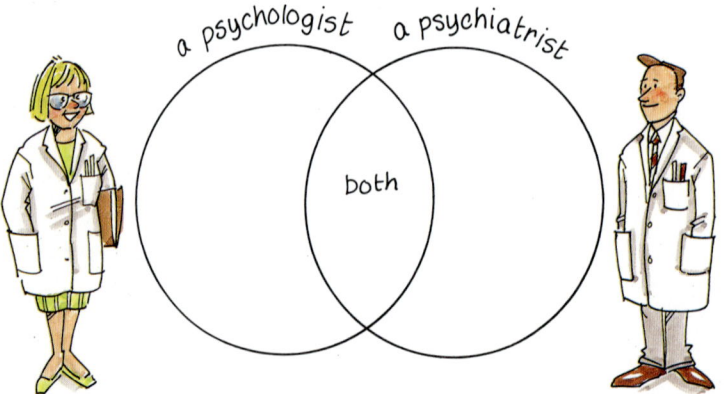

Compare your answers with the rest of the class.

3

1 In groups, compare the following definitions of 'personality'. Which do you prefer?

How a person is, feels, thinks and behaves.
The whole nature or character of a particular person.
The state of existing as a particular person.
What makes an individual, individual.

Do you have a definition of your own that you think is more appropriate?

2 Using circulating secretaries to take notes, discuss the following questions. Give reasons for your answers or examples from your own experience.

1 Do you think it's useful for people to know as much as they can about their personalities?
2 Do you think you have a fairly accurate idea of the sort of person you are?
3 'O wad some Pow'r the giftie gie us/To see ourselves as others see us!' Can you express this quotation in more modern language? What do you think about it?
4 Do you think personality plays an influential role in making important life decisions (e.g. deciding what sort of studies/work would be best for someone; deciding who to marry/live with, etc.)?
5 Do you think personality is shaped mainly by genetic or by environmental factors?
6 Do you think it's possible to change your personality?

Report back to the class.

4

1 As you read the following extract, think about how it relates to your conclusions in the previous discussion.

The ancient Greek philosophers had a phrase for it: 'Know yourself'. This is good advice. Because of our limited knowledge, it is difficult to make rational choices in education (What should I study?), in choosing a job (What occupation or profession should I go into?), in love (What sort of woman/man would I be happy with in marriage?), or indeed whenever we have to make some important decision about our futures. Professional psychologists see over and over again people who make the wrong choices, although it is quite obvious to the outsider that the choice is indeed very wrong; only too often this wrong choice is caused by erroneous self-perceptions, that is, a failure of the person concerned to 'know himself'. As Robert Burns expressed it so much more clearly:

O wad some Pow'r the giftie gie us
To see ourselves as others see us!
It wad frae mony a blunder free us
And foolish notion.

The passage you have just read is taken from a book called *Know Your*

Own Personality by H. Eysenck and G. Wilson. At the beginning of the book the authors give a historical account of the study of personality, starting with the ancient Greeks.

2 Read the second extract, and complete the comprehension check.

Before we can describe or measure personality, we must have some sort of model to represent it, and some sorts of concepts to encapsulate the different aspects of the model. The ancient Greeks used a *type* theory: indeed, the four types of the sanguine, the phlegmatic, the choleric and the melancholic man have passed into popular speech. The observations on which these descriptions were based were very astute; even now we can recognize particular types falling into these groups. But they were wrong in postulating that everyone would constitute an example of one type or the other; most people in fact combine aspects of two or more types, and thus fall between the four classificatory baskets. The theory of the four types had a long history, lasting for some two thousand years; it was not finally abandoned until the beginning of this century.

True or False?

1 The Greeks claimed that all people could be fitted into one or other of four categories of personality: the sanguine, the phlegmatic, the choleric or the melancholic person.
2 The Greek four-type theory of personality was very unsophisticated, and was quickly replaced by subsequent theories.
3 Modern psychologists believe that the Greek model was too rigid, and that most people are a mixture of types.

The Greek model of the four types of temperament can be represented like this:

3 In the Middle Ages, these four temperaments were called 'Humours'. Can you match the following definitions to the correct humour?

1 (Habitual or consitutional tendency to) sadness or depression; pensive sadness; (Hist.) one of the four Humours, black bile.

a CHOLER

2 Blood red (Hist.) of the temperament in which the blood predominates over the other Humours, with ruddy complexion and courageous hopeful amorous disposition . . . habitually hopeful, confident, expecting things to go well.

b MELANCHOLY

3 (Hist.) one of the four Humours, bile, anger, irascibility.

c PHLEGM

4 1. Thick, viscous semi-fluid substance secreted by mucous membranes of respiratory passages especially when morbid or excessive, and discharged by cough etc. 2. This substance regarded as a Humour; coolness, calmness, sluggishness, apathy.

d SANGUINE

5

1 Look at the words below. Do they have anything in common?

moody	rigid	responsive	changeable
pessimistic	touchy	impulsive	easygoing
carefree	lively	controlled	aggressive
sober	optimistic	sociable	talkative
outgoing	reserved	passive	active
calm	peaceful	leadership	thoughtful
quiet	restless	even-tempered	anxious
excitable	careful	unsociable	reliable

2 🖭 Listen to the conversation.

1 Write down the name given to the words in the above list, and what it means.

2 Tick any words mentioned by the speaker.

13

3 Work in groups of three or four.

  1 Discuss any words in the list that are new for you. Use a dictionary if no one in the group is sure of the meaning.

  2 The speaker said that certain words in the list tend to go together, such as 'sociable' and 'lively'; 'reserved' and 'quiet'. We can also see how these relate in some way to the four types of personality distinguished by the ancient Greeks as shown in exercise 4. 'Reserved' and 'quiet' go with 'melancholic'; 'sociable' and 'lively' go with 'sanguine' and so on. Try to put all the words in the list into an appropriate category. There are eight words in each category. Two have been done for you.

CHOLERIC	SANGUINE	PHLEGMATIC	MELANCHOLIC
touchy	sociable	careful	reserved
aggressive	lively	calm	quiet

When you have finished, compare your categories with those described in Figure A on page 86. What do you notice about its circular arrangement as compared with a linear arrangement? What additional information is given in Figure A?

  3 Using the words above, quickly write down three personality traits for each of the following.

    a the ideal boss

    b the ideal friend

    c the ideal partner

  Compare your views with one or two other people's.

6

1 How do modern psychologists find out about people's personalities? Try to complete the text below with your own ideas.

To find out what sort of personality someone has, modern psychologists generally use _____ which measure different _____. These are then grouped together under one general personality _____.

  But this modern use of the word does not imply rigid categories into which each of us fits perfectly. Rather, we would seem to be a _____. Furthermore, the word _____ is also used in the sense that there is a _____ from one extreme to the other, with most of us falling nearer the centre than the extremes.

2   As you listen to the interview, correct/complete the text.

7   **1**   Look at Figures 1 and 2.

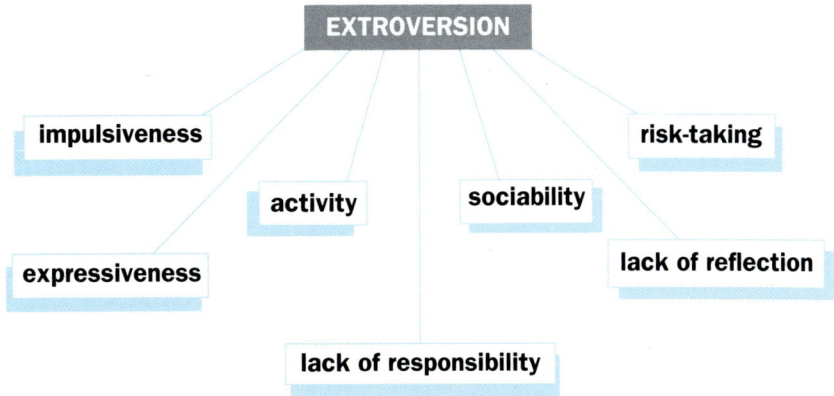

Figure 1

Figure 2

These represent two of the major personality typologies. You will now hear a description of the third major type. Tough-mindedness, and its opposite extreme, Tender-mindedness. Before you listen, do the task below.

Would you associate the following characteristics with someone who is 'tough' or someone who is 'tender'? Tick the appropriate column.

CHARACTERISTICS	TOUGH	TENDER
enjoys a fight	☐	☐
allows others to take advantage of him/her	☐	☐
likes to win	☐	☐
gets pleasure out of helping people	☐	☐
is not very adventurous	☐	☐
tries to convert others to his/her point of view	☐	☐
is frightened of snakes	☐	☐

2 🔲 As you listen . . .

1 Check the predictions you just made against what the speaker says about a tough-minded person.

2 Listen again and complete the subtraits in Figure 3 below. The first letter is given for you.

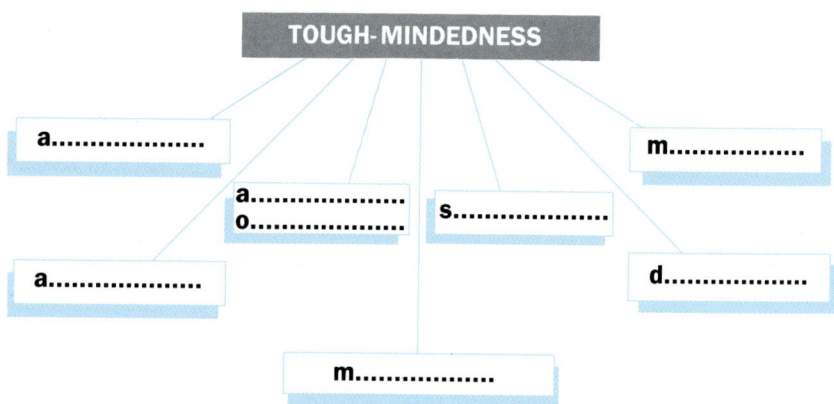

Figure 3

8 Look at the following words/expressions which you have seen in this unit. Can you remember what they mean? Can you use them in a sentence?

habitual	a fairly accurate idea	self-perceptions
touchy	shaped by	outgoing
astute	blunder	easygoing
encapsulate	fit into	furthermore

THINKING ABOUT LEARNING

9 This unit contains a lot of vocabulary. In groups discuss the following points.

1 Which is harder, remembering what a word means, or remembering how to use it?

2 Do you think it's necessary to make an effort to learn new vocabulary, or do you think it gets 'picked up' as you go along?

3 If you do make an effort to learn new vocabulary, what methods do you use?

4 How many people in the group have a) a bilingual dictionary b) a monolingual dictionary? What are the advantages/disadvantages of each?

5 How many people in the group are vocabulary freaks (secret dictionary readers, compulsive list makers, avid idiom hunters, etc.)? How many are allergic to vocabulary work (too boring, too time-consuming, etc.)?

UNIT 2 TESTING TESTING

1 **1** Complete the following questionnaire on your own. When you've finished, discuss your answers with two or three other people.

	AGREE	DISAGREE
It is impossible to get an accurate idea of someone's personality by using a written test.	☐	☐
The only reliable way of measuring a person's intellectual abilities is an IQ test.	☐	☐
An employer can get a better idea of a candidate through an interview rather than an impersonal written test.	☐	☐
Modern society has gone test mad.	☐	☐

2 ▱ On the tape you can hear Annie talking about a job interview she had in France. As you listen the first time, choose the correct answer below by ticking the appropriate box.

---

1 Annie's immediate reaction to the phrase 'personality tests' is
  favourable ☐ unfavourable ☐
2 She thinks the tests she took were
  too fast ☐ too slow ☐
3 Which of the following answers were allowed on the test?
  yes ☐   sometimes ☐
  perhaps ☐   no ☐
  don't know ☐ question mark ☐
4 Which of the following graphs was used to plot Annie's results?
  1 ☐   2 ☐   3 ☐

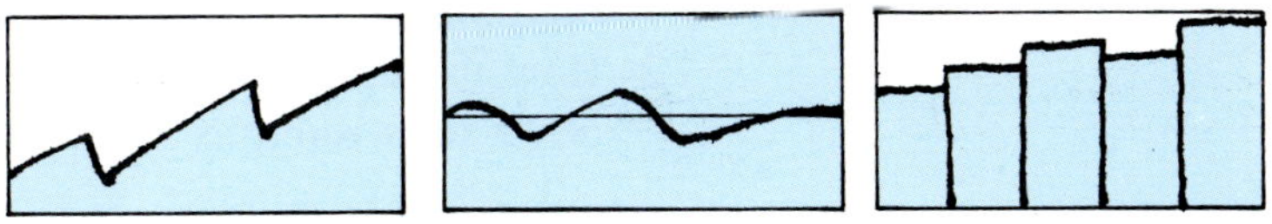

5 According to the test, Annie was
  indecisive   ☐   self-confident   ☐
  moody   ☐   easily-influenced   ☐
  submissive   ☐   tough-minded   ☐
  assertive   ☐   unable to take criticism   ☐
6 Annie took the tests
  seriously ☐ light-heartedly ☐

After listening, discuss your answers with a partner, putting a question mark by any areas of disagreement or uncertainty.

3 Read through the instructions below, and listen to the tape again.

1 Check any areas of uncertainty that arose from the first listening.
2 Complete these questions/statements mentioned by Annie.
   a Does the sight of bitten nails _____ ?
   b If you saw a bird with a broken wing _____?
   c Johnny thinks his father is _____ .
   d When Johnny got told off _____ .
3 What was Annie's reason for the ending she chose for **d** above?
4 What is Annie's final opinion about the test? (Try to note her exact words.)

Discuss your answers together before listening to the second part of the conversation.

4 😑 In this extract, you'll hear Tim's reactions to what Annie has just said. As you listen, complete the right-hand side of the diagram with Y (= yes), N(= no), or ? (= don't know). The first one is done for you.

FACTORS TAKEN INTO CONSIDERATION IN PSYCHIATRIC TESTING PROCEDURES	SAME FACTORS TAKEN INTO CONSIDERATION IN ANNIE'S INTERVIEW?
1 written test	Y
2 behavioural considerations	☐
3 history of the person being tested	☐
4 cultural factors	☐
5 qualifications of the person administering the test	☐

1 Discuss your answers with the class, giving reasons for your opinions.
2 How might cultural factors be important in personality and other tests, such as IQ tests?

5 😑 As you listen to the final part of Annie and Tim's conversation, try to imagine yourself in the role of the person who is being interviewed for the job. What would *you* do?

After listening to these short extracts, do you yourself get any ideas about Annie's personality? What influenced you?

Optional activity: Testing a Test (see instructions on page 80).

2

1 Before you read the extract that follows, look at the tests below.
  1 Work through them on your own.
  2 Compare your results with those of two or three other people.
  3 Discuss with your group what you think the tests are trying to measure.

Test 1

The different types of fruit have different values. Added together they give the totals shown. Work out the missing total for the left hand column.

Test 2

Which is the odd one out in each of the five boxes below?

Test 1

Test 2

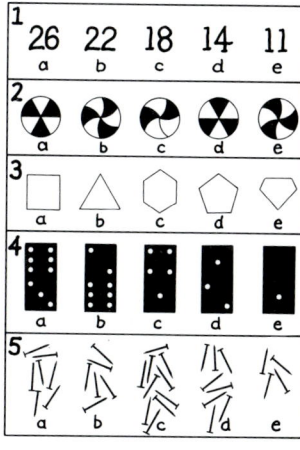

Test 3

Think of uses for bricks, and list as many as you can.

2 Contrary Imaginations

The following extract is from a book called *Contrary Imaginations* by Liam Hudson. The book is based on a study of British schoolboys in the 1960s in which Dr Hudson explores possible differences between what we might call 'the arts mind' and 'the science mind'. In the course of the study, he has some interesting things to say about the notions of 'intelligence' and 'creativity', and about what he calls 'convergence' and 'divergence'.

The conventional intelligence test is by now familiar. This usually consists of questions in the form of puzzles. The individual is set a problem to which he is required to find the right answer; and he is frequently invited to choose this right answer from a list of alternatives. The victim knows that there is one solution which is correct, and his task is to ferret it out. His reasoning is said to *converge* on to the right answer. A typical intelligence test question might run:
Brick is to house as plank is to …
orange, grass, egg, boat, ostrich
Only one of the five alternatives satisfactorily completes the analogy: 'boat'. Not all intelligence test questions rest on argument by analogy, nor are they all verbal, nor are they invariably in multiple choice form:

a) Which of the following words has the same meaning as the word on the left?
Correct … near, fair, right, poor, good.
b) Which is the odd one out … dog, cat, horse, chicken, cow?
c) Which number is missing from this series ?… 1, 2, 4, , 16.
d) Add the smallest of these fractions to the second largest … 7/8, 16/17, 1/6, 1/34, 2/3, 18/19

Intelligence test questions may also be diagrammatical: logical relations expressed in terms of patterns. And although most intelligence tests are massively biased towards the deductive, puzzle-solving type of reasoning, some (the Wechsler Adult Intelligence Scale, for example) include a wide range of material, aimed to assess general knowledge, vocabulary and such simple skills as immediate memory. Thus, even though the scope of the conventional intelligence test is not easily defined, it does seem that nearly every item in nearly every test does have one assumption in common: that each question has only one right answer.

Consider now a typical question from a 'creativity' test:

How many uses can you think of for a brick?

Here, the individual is invited to *diverge*, to think fluently and tangentially, without examining any one line of reasoning in detail. There are thousands of possible uses for a brick, and clearly people will differ widely both in the quantity and the quality of the uses they suggest. Here are two sets of answers: the first, it hardly needs saying, is more numerous, wittier and more ingenious than the second.

(*Brick*) To break windows for robbery, to determine depth of wells, to use as ammunition, as pendulum, to practice carving, wall building, to demonstrate Archimedes' Principle, as part of abstract sculpture, cosh, ballast, weight for dropping things in river, etc., as a hammer, keep door open, footwiper, use as rubble for path filling, chock, weight on scale, to prop up wobbly table, paperweight, as firehearth, to block up rabbit hole.

(*Brick*) For building, for throwing through window.

Vocabulary

ferret out: to seek out, search for
converge: behave like two lines which start wide apart, then narrow to the same point
massively biased: very strongly influenced in one direction
assess: evaluate, get an idea of
scope: the reach, or extent
diverge: opposite of 'converge': behave like two lines starting from the same point and opening out
tangentially: going off in different directions
ingenious: clever at inventing
cosh: heavy stick for hitting people
ballast: heavy material placed in boat to make it steady
rubble: waste pieces of brick, stone, etc.
chock: block of wood placed beneath a wheel to stop it from moving

After reading the text:

1 Discuss any parts which you found unclear.
2 Check your answers to the tests in question 1 (page 86). Are you convergent or divergent?

3 **1** Look at the two quotations below. Both refer to famous people. Brainstorm suggestions as to who they might be. (Clues: they were both male; the first one emigrated to America from Germany and lived this century; the second was British and lived in the 19th century.)

> " (He) was not particularly skilful in traditional mathematics, and his records in school and college were mediocre."

> " I have no great quickness of apprehension or wit... my power to follow a long and purely abstract train of thought is very limited; I should, moreover, never have succeeded with metaphysics or mathematics."

(Answers on page 86)

Both of the people referred to above were what might be called 'creative thinkers'. Big ideas occurred to them in flashes of insight, hunches, or 'Aha!' reactions. One writer defined the latter as 'the sudden hunch, the creative leap of the mind that 'sees' in a flash how to solve a problem in a simple way'. He continues: '(This) is something quite different from general intelligence. Recent studies show that people who possess a high 'Aha!' ability are all intelligent to a moderate level, but beyond that level there seems to be no correlation between high intelligence and 'Aha!' thinking.'

21

2   Working with two or three other people, discuss the notions of 'intelligence' and 'creativity'. List your ideas under the headings below. You may want to give the names of well-known people you consider to be either intelligent or creative, or both; or list some professions which you think demand either or both of these qualities. You may also wish to include expressions or definitions from the reading extracts.

INTELLIGENCE	CREATIVITY
_____	_____
_____	_____
_____	_____
_____	_____
_____	_____
_____	_____

3   ⌷ Listen to someone giving her views on the differences between intelligence and creativity. As you listen, add her ideas to the list.

4   Look up the definitions of 'intelligence' and 'creativity' in a dictionary. How do these definitions compare with the speaker's ideas and the ideas you listed?

5   Look at the following quotations on the subject of creativity. Tick those you agree with. Discuss your answers with two or three other people.
   1 Creativity is just for geniuses and artists.
   2 Instability is an intrinsic part of our lives, to deal with it we need to find creative solutions to the challenges of everyday life . . . creativity will be the survival skill of the nineties.
   3 Most of us have been taught that it's wrong to do things differently or look at things differently.

6 Working with a partner, try your hand at some 'Aha!' thinking.
Either: Try the Three-Bottle Problem on page 83. **Or:** Working with
a partner, try the problems below. Student A try to solve problem 1,
Quibble's Glasses; Student B try to solve problem 2, Steak Strategy. If
you succeed, explain the solution to your partner. If you get stuck,
turn to page 86.

Quibble's Glasses

*Barney, who works in a café, is
showing two of his customers
a puzzle that uses ten glasses.*

Barney *There are ten glasses
in this row, the first five are
filled with orange juice, the
next five are empty. Can you
move just four glasses to
make a row in which the full
and empty glasses alternate?*

Barney *That's right. Just
switch places with the second
and seventh glass, and with
the fourth and ninth.*

*Professor Quibble, who was
always thinking of tricky
solutions, happened to be
listening.*

Prof Quibble *Why four
glasses? I can do it by just
moving two glasses. Can't
you?*

Steak Strategy

*Mr Johnson has a small
outdoor grill just big enough to
hold two steaks. His wife, and
daughter Betsy, are hungry and
anxious to eat. The problem is
to grill three steaks in the
shortest possible time.*

Mr Johnson *Let's see. It takes
twenty minutes to grill both
sides of one steak because
each side takes ten minutes.
And since I can cook two
steaks at the same time,
twenty minutes will be enough
time to get two steaks ready.
Another twenty minutes will
grill the third steak and the job
will be done in forty minutes.*

Betsy *But you can do it much
faster, Daddy. I've just worked
out how you can save ten
minutes.*

*What clever 'Aha!' insight did
Betsy have?*

1 **Question:** Which of the two singers below was called by *Time* magazine 'the biggest star in the world'?

Answer: Both.
Question: Think of one word to describe what has changed in the Michael Jackson of today (picture on the right) compared with the Michael Jackson of 1979 (picture on the left).
Answer: Image.

Look at the pictures below and say how these people's images have changed.

2 In groups of three or four students, discuss the following questions. Use circulating secretaries to take notes.

1 What exactly do you understand by the word 'image'? How about 'self-image'?

2 How do people project a particular image? List all the different ways you can think of.

3 Choose two famous personalities with a strong image. Try to define what the image is, and how it is projected.

4 Why is image so important for media figures, like politicians, stars, etc?

5 Is image important only for well-known public figures? Is it important for you?

6 Does the idea of 'image' apply only to people? Can you think of other things which may have an image?

7 Do you sometimes try to project different images of yourself in different situations? Give examples.

Secretaries report back briefly to the class. Are there any points you wish to discuss further?

3

1 Imagine you are at a party. You are introduced to various guests who explain their jobs as follows:

1 I'm in advertising. 3 I'm a consultant.
2 I'm a copy-writer. 4 I work freelance.

What ideas would you have about the kind of work each person does? Discuss with your partner.

ADVERTISING BUDGET

THE
LINE

2 🖃 David works in the advertising business. As you listen to him talking about his job, complete the following tasks.

1 Look at the advertising budget on the left. Put the following things, mentioned by David, in their correct place – above the line or below the line.

a ⬚ sexy juicy jobs   b ⬚ radio   c ⬚ less interesting stuff   d ⬚ TV

2 Put a ring round the sort of copy-writing David does.

3 Which card has the right image?

David Pearl	David Pearl
Freelance Copy-writer	Creative Consultant

4 Match the following expressions with the appropriate card.
chief   stature
Indian   on the sidelines
wrong signals   distinguished

4   **Adventures in the Image Trade**

Read the first part of the article and answer the questions with a partner.

Part 1

When Dale Carnegie began teaching businessmen how to win friends and influence people back in 1910, he didn't talk much about "image". Today, firms with names like Communispond, Charismedia, and Mediacom offer to train business executives in the latest psychological techniques of "interpersonal communication". Most of these firms concentrate on public speaking, while others include it as part of a package called "total image".

1 Who was Dale Carnegie? If you don't know, are there any clues in the article to help you guess?

2 What do you think the reason is for choosing names like Communispond, Charismedia and Mediacom?

Part 2

What picture comes into your mind when you read the following phrase: 'he looked the very image of the successful executive'? Exchange ideas with a partner then read the second part of the article and compare the description with your impressions.

The writer goes to one of these management training courses.

The next morning, I joined my seminar-mates in the AMA classroom. We were greeted there by our instructor, Fred Knapp, a tall, square-jawed, handsome fellow with curly, graying hair and a deep, hearty voice. Wearing a three-piece dark gray suit, he looked the very image of the successful executive—the image we were supposed to acquire. A former sales executive with Sears, Knapp started his own consulting firm eight years ago, and now trains groups of executives at his office in New York or at corporate sites around the country.

Knapp asked each of us to come up to the front of the room and give a two-minute extemporaneous talk, which he videotaped, about ourselves and why we had come to this seminar. The 22 men and two women in our group ranged in age from their mid-30s to mid-50s, and in rank from middle-level manager to senior vice-president. The group included six sales executives from insurance companies, three from Monsanto's agricultural-chemicals division, an auto-parts plant manager, a regional manager for a large convenience-store chain, a management-training director, a regional loan officer for a bank, and a credit manager for a pizza-cheese company.

While a few of these people had decided to come to the seminar on their own, most had been sent by their companies as part of their management training. Some admitted that they'd been sent because of an "image problem". Among the reasons given: "to gain more self-confidence", "to learn how to deal with people without being self-conscious", "to learn how to present myself favourably to my superiors", "to get an edge in dealing with our suppliers", "to help myself grow into a leadership position". One man had come because his boss had insisted: "He thinks I need it, and I guess he's right". Another fellow said, "At 5 foot 3 and 120 pounds, I feel I need all the help I can get in projecting a positive image." A 52 year-old vice-president told us, "I used to have more self-confidence years ago, in a lower-level position, than I do now. I feel I have the ability to achieve things, but I have trouble projecting that ability."

Glossary

square-jawed: the jaws are the bones forming the framework of the mouth, running up to the ears; some people have a square, definitely marked lower jaw giving an impression of strength and determination

hearty voice: strong, clear, good-humoured, sincere voice

corporate sites: company premises (e.g. offices, factories)

extemporaneous: without preparation

rank: position in a scale of responsibility, quality, social status

an edge: an advantage

Quick round-the-class quiz.

1 How many people were there on the course?
2 How many different professions can you remember?
3 What was the age-range of the participants?
4 What were some of the reasons given for coming on the course?

Glossary

a disarmingly plaintive quality: a rather sad and moving quality which makes the listener sympathetic

bluff façades: a frank, blunt, hearty outward appearance, giving the impression of being in control

inadequacy; incompetence; the inability to do the job properly

grads: graduates; students leaving university after their final exams

old-boy networks: a system by which people (mainly men) get jobs because they have been to the same school, or moved in the same social circles, as the boss

credentials: evidence of achievement (e.g. qualifications, diplomas, work-experience)

As you read Part 3, think about how the writer associates the idea of 'change' with feelings of insecurity.

Part 3

These confessions of insecurity had a disarmingly plaintive quality—honest and painful admissions that beneath the bluff façades these managers displayed back at the office, many were troubled by feelings of vulnerability and inadequacy. In their brief personal stories, many revealed, indirectly, the sources of their insecurity: farm boys who had to adjust to big-city business; field representatives who were promoted to corporate headquarters; older men threatened by aggressive young business-school grads; women whose success had brought them up against their companies' old-boy networks; technical or research people moving into administrative or sales positions. The common factor seemed to be change—from a setting in which success had been proved, to one in which one's credentials and reputation had to be re-established. It wasn't necessarily that they had climbed above their level of competence, but that they had moved out of the culture in which they felt at ease into one in which they felt insecure. Knapp played to this insecurity, telling us that the main problem was not our self-image, but our "exterior image"—how others perceive us. "Do you look in charge of yourself? If not, you have a credibility gap."

Part 4 ☺

Look at the drawings below. Put a tick next to the ones you think Knapp would advise.

As you listen, put a tick next to the pictures which most closely match Knapp's suggestions. What are your reactions?

How to improve your executive image

The best way to stand

The correct way to wear a jacket

| Every 15–30 seconds | Every 30 seconds | Every 15 seconds |

The correct timing of hand gestures

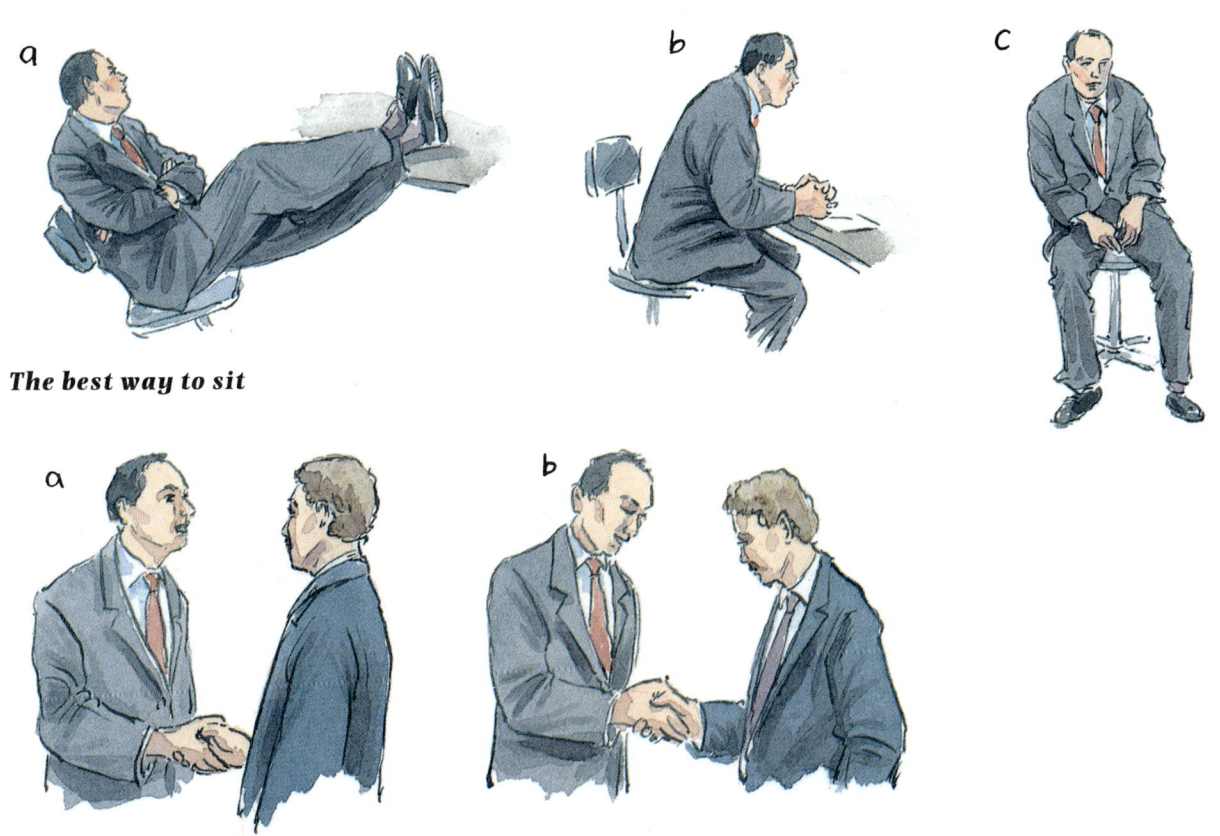

The best way to sit

The correct way to shake hands

Part 5 🔲

1 After the course, the writer telephoned Harris Blum, the director of an executive-recruiting firm in New York and asked him for his views on the current preoccupation with the idea of executive image. Listen to the tape and say whether Blum was for or against these training sessions.

2 What exactly did Blum tell him? Listen again, and see if you can re-phrase his colloquial answer.

3 Think of someone you know well. How does that person use 'body language' to convey what he or she is feeling? How do you know, without being told, that the person is feeling bored, annoyed, sympathetic, etc?

5 Other images

1 What do you understand by the expression 'corporate image'? Look at the advertisement below. What sort of company is being advertised? What sort of image is being suggested?

What do you need to transplant a human organ?

Anaesthetics, blood plasma, oxygen and aviation fuel.

Aviation fuel? Think about it.

Before someone flies the donor organ to its new owner, someone has to fly to fuel the aircraft.

Four men from BP's aviation staff recently received awards for doing just that.

A pilot from the St John's Ambulance Brigade's Air Wing explains:

"Not long ago, I got a call at 1 a.m. to fly a kidney to Glasgow," he says. "One of the Air BP staff got straight out of his warm bed, drove from his home at Porthcawl about 20 miles away, took a tanker out of the depot, and fuelled my aircraft.

By 2 a.m. I was in the air."

As you can see, there's more to running an oil company than simply pumping petrol into motor cars.

Britain at its best.

---

2 🔲 David talks about corporate image. Read the questions first.

1 In what way did he have to act as a therapist when creating an image for the property company? (These expressions may help you: different personalities/dreams/coincide/steer a path/put their backs up.)

2 What identity did he design for the accountancy company? Rearrange the words in the label.

> **COMPANY OF COMMON GOT ALL THE TOUCH OUR A MULTINATIONAL HAS THE RESOURCES YET AND WE'VE**

3 How does David think his new visiting card has changed him?

4 How does he see the next change in his image?

5 How do you think he would have answered question 7 in your discussion on page 25? (Do you sometimes project different images of yourself in different situations?)

6 What are your reactions to this interview?

After listening, answer the questions with a partner.

3 *Time* magazine, reporting the repairs carried out to the Statue of Liberty, called the statue 'a perfect emblem of America's self-image: colossal, principled, generous.' Do you agree that this is how Americans think of their country? Does it match the image that you have of America?

What about your own country? Does it have a self-image? In what way might this be different from its exterior image?

THINKING ABOUT LEARNING

6 'Children who learn co-operatively (compared with those who learn competitively or independently) learn better, feel better about themselves and get along better with each other'.

In groups of three or four, discuss the following points.

1 What do you think is meant by learning 'co-operatively' rather than 'competitively or independently'?
2 Have you used a co-operative approach for any of the activities in this book? If so, what are your conclusions?
3 Can you think of ways in which you could help other learners in your group, or in which they could help you?

UNIT 4 STEREOTYPES

1 Choose the best answer.

> A stereotype is . . . a hi-fi fanatic
> a dictaphone for secretaries
> other

Look at the following definition. Do you find it amusing? What does the intended humour rely on?

> Heaven is where the police are British, the cooks are French, the mechanics German, the lovers Italian and it is all organized by the Swiss. Hell is where the chefs are British, the mechanics French, the lovers Swiss, the police German, and it is all organized by the Italians.

2

1 Working with a partner, try to list all the member states of the EEC. Compare your list with the rest of the class.
2 In 1984, just before the elections for the European Parliament, a French magazine published a cartoon like the one opposite.
The member states at that time were: Denmark, Belgium, Germany, Luxembourg, Greece, the UK, France, Holland, Republic of Ireland and Italy. Below are the ten stereotypes attributed by the cartoonist to these various members. Working with a partner, try to decide which stereotype he put with which nationality. (Answers on page 87)

discreet prolific serious   elegant   calm
funny   gallant   disciplined hospitable virile

 WHO IS...

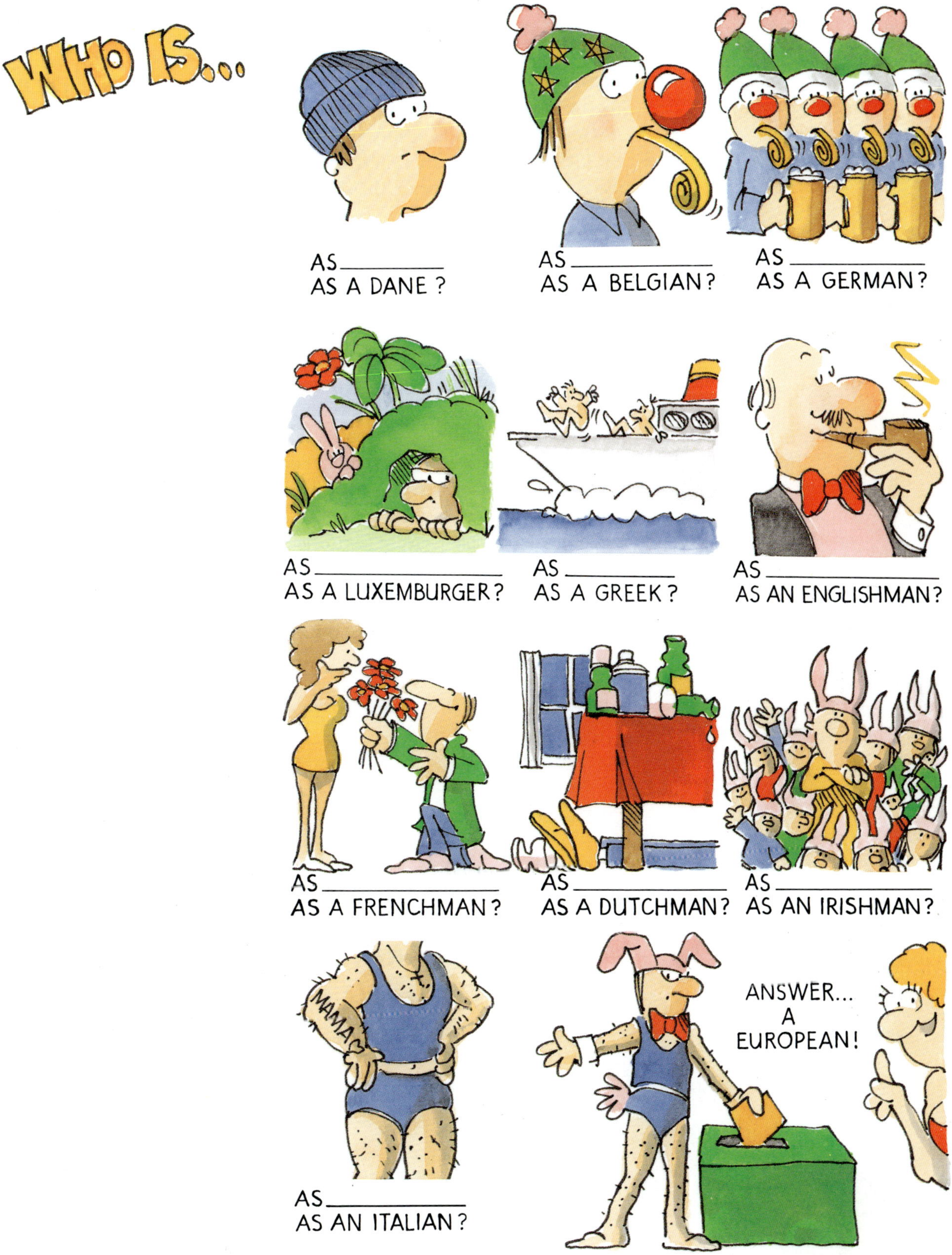

AS _____
AS A DANE ?

AS _____
AS A BELGIAN ?

AS _____
AS A GERMAN ?

AS _____
AS A LUXEMBURGER ?

AS _____
AS A GREEK ?

AS _____
AS AN ENGLISHMAN ?

AS _____
AS A FRENCHMAN ?

AS _____
AS A DUTCHMAN ?

AS _____
AS AN IRISHMAN ?

AS _____
AS AN ITALIAN ?

ANSWER...
A EUROPEAN !

3

1 Working with two or three other people, think of four or five nationalities and brainstorm common stereotypes that you have heard people use about them.

2 Working on your own, quickly write down five or six stereotypes for your own nationality.

3 Compare your findings for 1 and 2 with the rest of the class and list them on the board. Which stereotypes are positive, which negative and which neutral? Does this tell us anything about stereotypes?

4 Do the following questionnaire on your own. When you've finished, discuss your answers with the rest of the class.

A = I agree   B = I'm not sure   C = I disagree

		A	B	C
1	National stereotypes are dangerous because they provoke racial prejudice.	☐	☐	☐
2	Stereotypes contain a certain amount of truth.	☐	☐	☐
3	There is no such thing as 'national character' and therefore the idea of national stereotypes is rubbish.	☐	☐	☐
4	The reason stereotypes exist is because people are afraid of diversity, change, and what is unknown. They prefer to cling to simple classifications which maintain an old, familiar and established order.	☐	☐	☐
5	Stereotypes are simply harmless sorts of jokes we tell about other nationalities or groups of people.	☐	☐	☐

4

1 Draw lines from the adjectives to the names of the animals you think they might describe.

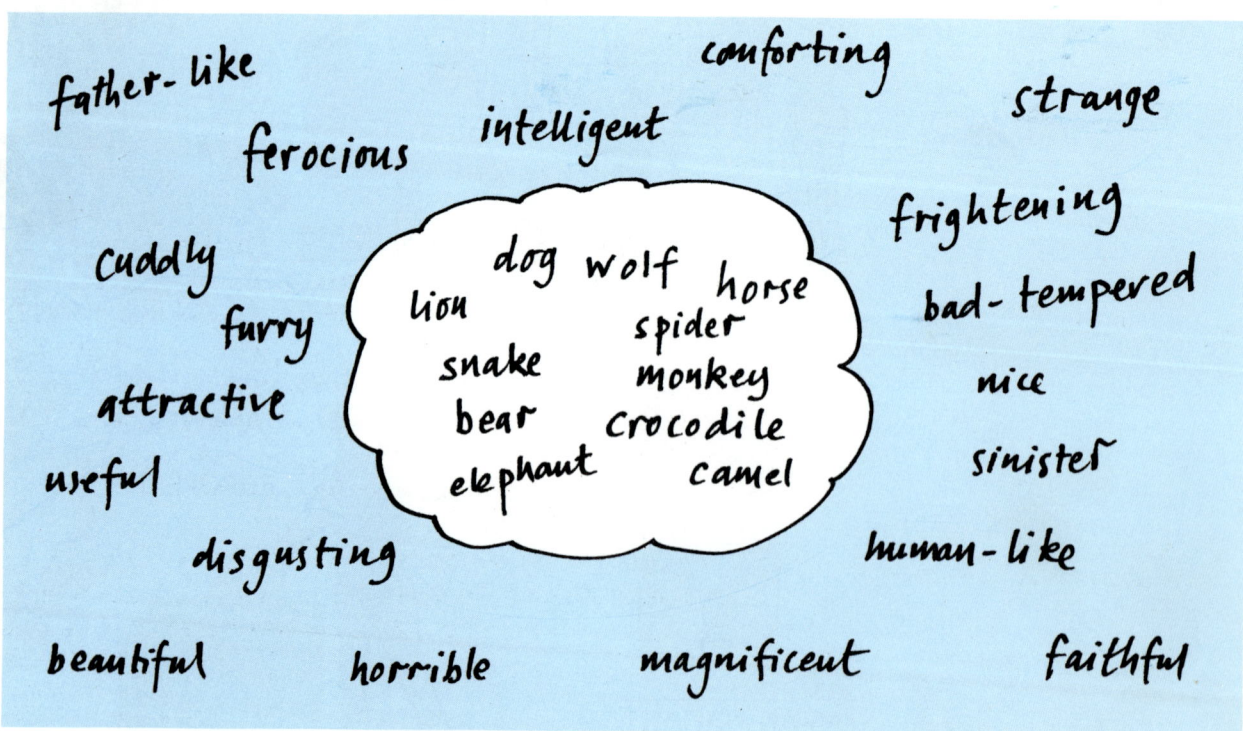

father-like   comforting   strange

ferocious   intelligent

frightening

cuddly   bad-tempered

furry

attractive   nice

useful   sinister

disgusting   human-like

beautiful   horrible   magnificent   faithful

dog wolf horse lion spider snake monkey bear crocodile elephant camel

Compare your ideas with a partner. Do you agree?

2 ☺ Mike is talking about the questionnaire in exercise 3. He is particularly interested in the fourth statement, but he relates it to animal rather than human stereotypes. As you listen, complete the table below with the animals he mentions, and the reasons that children like or dislike them.

ANIMALS LIKED	REASON

ANIMALS DISLIKED	REASON

3 Listen again, and note the reasons for his interest. He uses the terms 'chaos', 'world picture' and 'value systems'.

5 National stereotypes, animal stereotypes . . . in groups of three or four try to write down as many other stereotypes you can think of. Don't show your list to the other groups. Give a description of one of the stereotypes on your list (but not the name of the group or thing it refers to) to the other groups in the class. They should try to guess the name from the description.

6 **1** Stereotypes are often used in advertising. Before reading the passage on the next page, sort the following stereotypes into two lists, male and female, and try to work out what they mean. Which are positive and which are negative?

omnipotent tycoon, vamp, sultry sex pot,
handsome hulk, wonder mum, brainless drudge, super stud

Compare you ideas with your partner.

2 Find the correct order for a) the words of the headline, b) the different parts of the text.

Much than a face more pretty

We have erred, he told them. We have followed the media stereotypes and depicted women as sultry sex pots or brainless drudges. "It wasn't all our fault: others created the stereotype but we repeated it and went on repeating it because we didn't think it mattered."

But so far, the new advertising for the new woman has proved as hilariously hamfisted as the early Katies of the Oxo ads. The best examples, naturally, come from the United States but we too have already seen harbingers of what Mr Day calls the "mops-into-attaché-cases stereotype" or "working women chic".

buy tomato soup, the ads now show a man with that special look of loony ecstasy, grabbing at the life-saving tin that used to stand between a woman and failure as a wife and mother.

It would be niggardly to scoff at the efforts of Barry Day and people like him. I have no doubt at all that the daily repetition of traditional advertising images of women have a powerful reinforcing influence on everyone exposed to them. It therefore matters quite a lot whether

they are more or less daft or degrading. If top executives with power to change things are bothering to stop and re-examine their attitudes with a sincere concern to get it right, one ought to be glad, not to say grateful. But there is a huge flaw in the argument.

As Barry Day himself admits, advertising must use stereotypes because people in television or newspaper commercials must speak to a mass audience in the simplest of language. All that even the most enlightened and unsexist of agencies can do, therefore, is to make the stereotypes a bit less crass.

The women in these ads are dungareed visions of loveliness, whirling through a high-speed day to sell glamour—perfume or clothes—in a new language. Or they are senior vice-presidents (the uniform here is a white tailored suit with silk blouse) ripe for the new women's market of insurance and banking services. The best of Mr Day's examples was a musical comedy number in which a gladsome girl re-enacts the traditional broken-down car scene, but instead of ending in rescue by a handsome hulk, she is seen triumphantly mending the fan belt with her panty hose.

Beware, says Mr Day, who has spent three hours talking to America's leading feminist writers and so is alert to every man-trap. Beware, we are doing it all again. We are making a new and equally insulting stereotype. And he is right. What is more, since someone has to

THERE IS no one in the world more concerned, scrupulous and perceptive about the "new woman" than a really good advertising executive. That may be partly due to embarrassment at what the really bad ones have been up to for the last 20 years, but it is also becoming commercially essential.

Barry Day, President of the respected McCann agency, has devoted much time and thought to the images of women projected by advertisements and in finding out how they are received by the independent, post-pill working women of the 1980s. Last week, he gave an illustrated presentation on the subject to members of the Advertising Association.

Mr Day and his colleagues are well aware that women have changed, that whether they work at home or outside it, their status, self-image and economic power are becoming increasingly independent and most important of all, their dreams and aspirations are not quite the same as they were in the 1950s. The advertising men are now cudgelling their market research figures for an answer to Freud's question: What does a woman want? The blunt ones ask because it holds the clue to what they can sell her and how. Others mingle their commercial considerations with a feeling that advertising has some kind of moral or social duty not to insult or demean women. Motives, however do not much matter: the end result is the same.

3 The author mentions old, or traditional female stereotypes, and new, modern ones. Complete the columns below with specific examples of these from the article.

OLD STEREOTYPES	NEW STEREOTYPES

4 The writer continues:

> Women complain about the way they are portrayed by advertising, but what of the images of men? Made by a male-dominated industry, without any nefarious urge to oppress, they are just as idiotic, just as exploitative, just as wedded to the stereotypes of the super stud and the omnipotent tycoon as images of women are to the vamp and the wonder mum.

The article was written in 1980. Working in groups of three or four, complete the following tasks.

1 List any new, recent stereotypes of men that you have noticed in TV or cinema advertisements.
2 Collect examples of new stereotypes from magazines.
3 Are there different stereotypes of men and women in the advertisements in your own country? Make a list.

When you've finished, compare your conclusions with the other groups.

5 Look at these photographs from a recent magazine article. The title was 'The Ad World's New Bimbos'. What is a bimbo? What was the main point the article was making, in your opinion?

7

1 Did anyone include singers in the lists you made in exercise 5 on page 35? Look at the different types of singer and match them to the adjectives you would expect to apply to them. You may also add adjectives of your own.

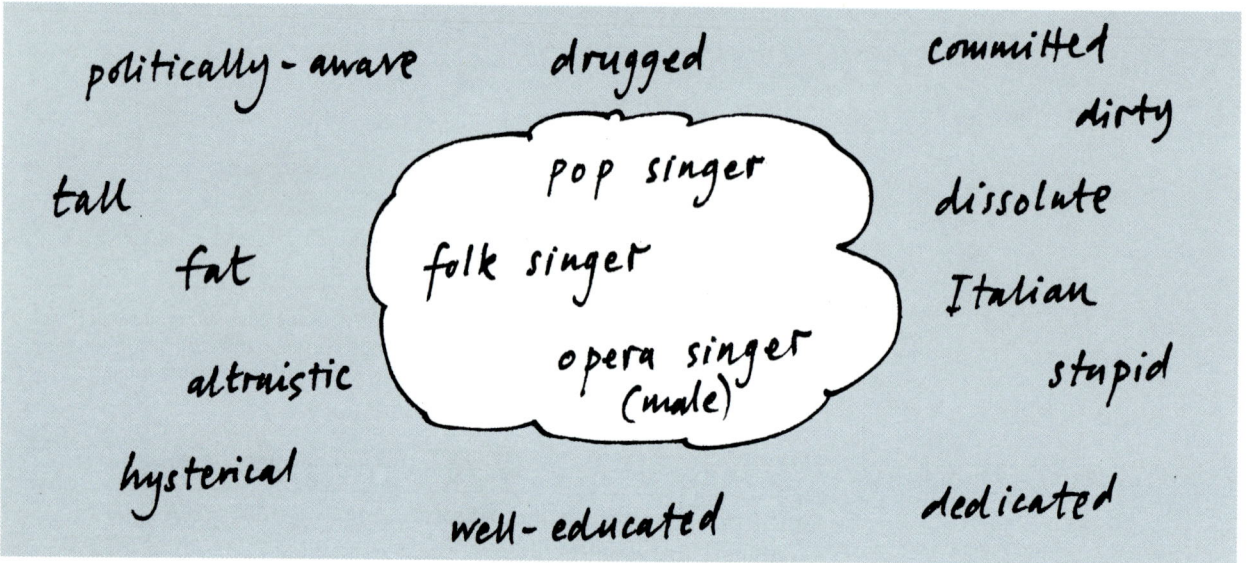

When you've finished, compare with a partner and see if you agree.

2 David sometimes has to go to desperate lengths to convince people that he is a singer. As you listen, answer the following questions.

1 What sort of singer is he?
2 What sort of discrepancies exist between the way David looks, and the way people expect him to look? Complete the table below.

DAVID	A STEREOTYPICAL...

3 Here are the 'English' words for different types of voices. Which language do they come from? Enter the words on the chart according to how high the voices are, and whether they refer to women singers or men.

Soprano   Bass   Baritone   Mezzo-soprano   Counter-tenor
Contralto   Tenor

	WOMEN	MEN
High		
Low		

UNIT 5 CLOTHES POWER

1

1 Think of sentences to illustrate the way the following verbs are used.

to wear	to undress
to clothe	to dress up
to overdress	to dress down
to dress	to cross dress

2 In pairs, match the adjectives on the left with a suitable clothes item on the right. In some cases more than one link can be made, e.g. shoes can be 'low-heeled' or 'lace-up'.

knee-length	shoes
high-necked	trousers
flesh-coloured	shirt
low-heeled	skirt
skin-tight	dress
lace-up	shoes
loose-fitting	blouse
body-hugging	tights

Discuss their meaning with your partner.

3 In groups of three or four, discuss the following questions, using circulating secretaries to make notes. Report back to the class when you've finished.

1 Would you say that you were someone who was interested in fashion?
2 Is what you wear important to you? Why/why not?
3 Do you always wear what you want, when you want?
4 Do you think that clothes express people's personality, or disguise it?
5 Describe the clothes in which you feel most comfortable, and 'yourself'.
6 Do you think that women on the whole are more interested in fashion than men?

2

1 Before you listen, discuss with your partner what you would wear in the following situations.

1 a job interview for a position with an advertising company
2 a dinner with an old friend that could turn into a romance
3 an interview with your bank manager to ask for a loan
4 a rock concert
5 a dinner (informal) at an old friend's house, with other old friends present

2 On the tape you'll hear Mike talking about the quotation below.

> *Clothes are a billboard of the self. They express dreams and disguises, rank and status, pride and dismay. Without them we are vulnerable, and largely anonymous: with them we are clad in an armour of cloth.* Harris Dienstfrey

Before you listen to his comments, what do *you* think about the quotation? Write your reactions in the table below.

YOUR REACTIONS	MIKE'S REACTIONS
	1 Initial reaction . . .
	2 Modified reaction . . .
	3 Final reaction . . .

In the course of the discussion, Mike's reactions to the quotation changed. As you listen, make notes on these changes in the table above.

3 Before you listen to the next part of the interview, work with a partner to find examples of clothing which might express the notions listed in the quotation. Write them in the table below.

YOUR EXAMPLES

Dreams _____

Disguises _____

Rank _____

Status _____

Pride _____

Dismay _____

_____

MIKE'S EXAMPLES

Dreams _____

Disguises _____

Rank _____

Status _____

Pride _____

Dismay _____

_____

As you listen, make notes on Mike's examples.

After you have listened:

1 Compare the various examples that you thought of and those mentioned by Mike.
2 Can you remember in what context he used the following expressions? overstated/dressing up/to stand out/subjective/highly thought of/ephemeral/stick to the suit/showing off

Discuss your answers with the rest of the class. What idea do you get of Mike's personality through a) the opinions he expresses and b) the way he speaks (voice, speed, choice of words, etc.)?

3

1 In groups of three or four, discuss the following quotation.

> 'All choices of clothing, particularly the quick and simple ones, involve allying oneself with others who have made the same choice.'
> Anne Hollander, *Seeing Through Clothes*.

2 **Either** Imagine you are sitting at a table outside a café, watching people pass by. How many different 'groups' can you identify, just by their clothing?

Or Make notes on the different clothes worn by the members of the class. How many different 'groups' can you find?

Optional activity: Simulation (see instructions, page 83).

4 **Dressing the Truth**

1 Before you read the article:
  1 Try the Back to Back game. Choose two students to go out of the room for two or three minutes then turn to page 87 for the rules.
  2 Discuss together possible meanings for the following expressions.
  personal image management   dressing for effect
  non-verbal communication   appearances matter

2 Read the article and make notes on what the author says about the above expressions. Discuss your answers with the rest of the class. Decide whether or not you think he would have agreed with the quotation on page 41 ('Clothes are a billboard of the self . . .'). Note anything he says which supports your opinion.

Most people say they wear what they do for practical reasons such as comfort or warmth. But the truth is more complex. Like it or not, our clothes are personal statements – and we might not always mean what they say.

Those of us who live surrounded by strangers – which in Britain in the 20th century is increasingly the norm – have to develop our skills of non-verbal communication in what the sociologist Irving Goffman has called *The Presentation of Self in Everyday Life*. Just as people have differing abilities in most things, there are obviously experts in this art – the geniuses of the street who can spot a genuine Rolex or a pair of original Levi 501s at 100 yards. But it is also true that *all of us* require basic skills to enable us to read the messages of the walking billboards around us and, just as importantly, to select appropriate items for use in our own personal image management.

These personal advertisements are not necessarily 'legal, decent, honest and truthful'. If asked to check out the claims made by our walking billboards, the Advertising Standards Authority would probably take most of us to court. We dress to impress, to confuse and to deceive (if only ourselves). Whether we utilize the skills of an undercover cop to blend into our surroundings or those of a pop star to stand out, there is generally a considerable gap between what we project in our appearance and the reality of our situation in life. It may be only when dressing for, say, a job interview or a first date that we are aware of our capacity for visual deceit but we are, in fact, at it all the time.

Dressing for effect is a game we all play. It is also a very serious business – not just in the sense that the clothing and make-up industries are big business (clothing manufacture is Britain's fourth biggest employer) but also because our own personal, economic, social and romantic relationships so often derive from effective image management. Except for the minority of people who live out their lives in small, rural communities where everyone knows everyone else, we inevitably build our relationships upon a foundation of fleeting initial visual encounters. It is a cliché that 'Appearances Matter' but it is none the less true. At a party, on the street, in the office, at a disco, when visiting a bank manager, verbal communication is only one aspect of our interaction – and frequently (perhaps surprisingly) it is often the least important source of information. How many important relationships in all our lives would have never developed to the verbal level if we had not surmounted the initial hurdle of visual compatibility?

The other side of the coin is our ability to interpret the appearances of others in order to avoid unpleasant or even dangerous encounters. On a dark, sparsely populated street the distant glimpse of a 'dodgy looking character' may make us cross to the other side or even retreat in the opposite direction – often without justification. Our prejudices about appearances frequently interfere with our logic. Muggers, pick-pockets, rapists and con-men rarely, in real life, look like the stereotypes we expect. Usually it is only very subtle inconsistencies of style and manner that are the clues we should look out for.

And if the interpretation of appearances is a complex game, the task of projecting to the world our own personal self-advertisement is no less so. Buying a new wardrobe – or even a pair of socks – is no easy matter, but the choices we make (yes, even in socks) are among our most important decisions. Many people who have abundant skills at anything from computer programming to writing pop songs are held back in life because they have never taken the time to develop their skills of image management. Yet it is not difficult to do so.

The first point to grasp is that items of clothing, make-up, hairstyles, etc. are *symbols*. Just as in learning the vocabulary of a foreign language, one has to learn the meanings of these everyday style symbols. Unfortunately there are no dictionaries of these things (their meanings are too ephemeral for that) but simply by taking note of what other people are 'saying' with what garments, you can become fluent enough to begin to evaluate what you are communicating through your own appearance.

To make this process a little easier, we present here in graphic form some of the things which people frequently attempt to communicate through the medium of their appearance, and invite you to consider how you and people you know fit into this scheme of things. Remember: What we illustrate here are the extremes – most of us fall somewhere in between them on a graduated scale.

The messages which we *think* we are transmitting are often not the ones which others actually read in our appearance. Get someone else to evaluate you. Then, independently evaluate yourself and compare your appearance profiles.

Do not expect the message which you are sending out to correspond to your real life situation. The presentation of self is the act of creating a public fiction about a character who happens to have your name. The only thing that matters is whether the fiction which you project is the one which you want the world to read.

Glossary

the norm: normal, or standard thing or situation

an undercover cop: a detective in disguise

we are at it all the time: we do it all the time

derive from: come from, originate in

fleeting: swift and temporary, ephemeral

surmounted the initial hurdle of . . .: managed to overcome their first obstacle of . . .

sparsely populated: with not many people about

a dodgy looking character: a suspicious looking person

muggers: people who attack and rob others (usually pedestrians)

con-men: 'confidence men', people who trick or cheat people by playing on their good faith or confidence

garment: an article of clothing

this scheme of things: this particular way of organizing or looking at life

a graduated scale: a scale with degrees of measurement which increase/decrease gradually

3 Look at the following description of a clothing style taken from the article: 'Trendy means anything which is in fashion'. Working with your partner, look at the two lists below. One list contains classifications, like 'trendy'; the other contains definitions, like 'anything which is in fashion'.

1 Match the classifications with the definitions.
2 Sort them into pairs of opposites, e.g. hard and soft.
3 Match them to the pictures.

CLASSIFICATIONS

1 Trendy means . . .
2 Soft means . . .
3 Body-dressing means . . .
4 Elitist means . . .
5 Hard means . . .
6 Traditional means . . .
7 Mind-dressing means . . .
8 Conformist means . . .
9 Egalitarian means . . .
10 Individual means . . .

DEFINITIONS

A casual, pastel shades, muted patterns, fussy, fine fabrics, lace, floral prints, frills, bows, suede, mohair and ribbons.

B work clothes, army surplus, practical fabrics, donkey jackets, Dr Martens, overalls, badges.

C 'normal' clothes which do not stand out and attract attention. Anything bought from a chain store will generally do the trick.

D whatever is unusual, unconventional, personal and distinctive.

E expensive fabrics, bespoke tailoring, couture, hand-made shoes, the family jewels, formal dress

F sportswear, dance clothes, muscle T-shirts, body-hugging stretch fabrics, suntan.

G tailored, sharp, angular, severe, minimalist, strong solid colours, bold stripes, pointed collars, black leather, studs and metal trimming.

H classic — anything which is timeless and does not date.

I loose-fitting, carelessly assembled, slightly rumpled clothes which do not show much flesh, briefcase bulging with books, spectacles.

J anything which is in fashion.

2

3

Are you reading me?

When you have finished, look at the messages below. With your partner, try to decide which classification goes with which message. The first one is done for you.

1 The message is: 'I'm efficient, businesslike, sharp, strong, aggressive, decisive, urban, sophisticated and in control.' = *hard*

2 The message is: 'I'm an intellectual, concerned with ideas not appearances, reasoning, rational, thoughtful, civilized and introspective.'

3 The message is: 'I'm a proud proletarian, salt of the earth, left wing, "Up the workers".'

4 The message is: 'I'm caring, nice, gentle, friendly, relaxed, innocent, passive and rural.'

5 The message is: 'I'm special, unique, creative, one in a million.'

6 The message is: 'I'm fit, sensual, instinctual, natural, intuitive.'

7 The message is: 'I'm a team player, one of the boys/girls – average, conventional and middle-of-the-road. I blend with my surroundings.'

8 The message is: 'I'm a member of an exclusive coterie, not one of the hoi polloi.' *hoi polloi* = the common people, the masses

9 The message is: 'I'm up-to-the-minute, going places, not stuck in a rut, progressive and in with the in crowd.'

10 The message is: 'I'm a pillar of the community – moral, upright, honest, God-fearing, worthy, honourable and virtuous.'

So . . . which one are you?

Optional activity: Choosing a Party Outfit (see instructions, page 85)

5   **THINKING ABOUT LEARNING**

In groups look at the following saying.
'The optimist sees only the doughnut, whereas the pessimist sees only the hole.'

In the dialogue below, imagine you are having lunch with the class pessimist. As you chat, try to give the 'optimistic' replies to his/her pessimistic view of group discussions.

Classmate *Boring. That's what it is. Plain boring. Sitting round with a group of people talking about things that nobody's the least bit interested in.*

You . . . .
. . . .
. . . .

Classmate *Well, anyway, even if you do manage to dredge up some remotely interesting subject, what are you supposed to say about it? I mean, either everybody in the group says 'Yes, I agree. In which case you might as well all go and have a coffee, or else you get one of these argumentative types who says, 'Well, actually, that's not what I think at all.' In which case you might as well still go and have a coffee, because if he disagrees, he disagrees, and you're not going to make him change his mind, are you? You might just as well say, 'Oh. Alright.', and shut up.*

You . . . .
. . . .
. . . .

Classmate *And another thing, so many of these discussions are so personal — I don't want to go around baring my soul to people I hardly know!*

You . . . .
. . . .
. . . .

Classmate *Well, quite apart from anything else, how on earth can you have a civilized discussion with someone you can't stand. That woman in my group! Well, I say my group, I know we change around a lot but I always seem to end up sitting next to her! You know the one I mean — she has the definitive opinion on everything! The meaning of the universe? She can tell you in three words. The best recipe for moussaka? She's got it in her recipe file, which just happens to be in her handbag. And then there's that totally pretentious bloke — what's his name? — the one who's always cheerful and smiling and ready to lend you a piece of paper and always going on about international co-operation and the future of humanity and stuff like that. In fact, when I come to think of it, I don't like anybody in the group very much, except you, of course. By the way, thanks for inviting me to this place — I usually just have a sandwich on my own, in the park.*

You . . . .
. . . .
. . . .

Classmate *Look, alright, let's ignore things like boring subjects and boring people, and let's look at the basic reason why we're here – to learn English, right? Right. So, how much English am I going to learn listening to some French guy or some Japanese guy or some German woman?*

You . . . .
. . . .
. . . .

Classmate *Well, OK, maybe you have a point. But let me just ask you one more thing: why has the waitress brought you a glass of wine that's half full while mine is half empty?*

UNIT 6 ADVERTISING

1 Look at the pictures below and try to guess what product is being advertised.

1

She was a dental assistant from Lewisham.
How did she get where she is today?

2

3

4

(Answers on page 87)

2

1 Advertisers always have a target market. Match the products with the most likely markets.

PRODUCT	POSSIBLE MARKET
unisex jeans	trendy young people between 20–35
eye-wrinkle cream	office managers
word processors	women over 35
low alcohol beer	environmentalists
cheap package holidays	middle to low income families
bio-degradable washing-up liquids	men over 45

Compare your ideas with a partner. Do you agree?

2 You will hear three advertisements. As you listen, complete the box below.

	1	2	3
ADVERTISEMENT FOR ...?			
MARKET AIMED AT?			
TECHNIQUES USED? (music/voice quality/ sex roles, etc.)			
LANGUAGE USED? (slang/colloquial/ literary/jargon, etc.)			

Discuss your ideas with the rest of the class.

3 **Popular Cocktails Competition**

A well-known vodka manufacturer once ran a competition in which entrants were asked to depict (in oils, crayon, embroidery or whatever) what the names of six vodka cocktails meant to them. The winners were chosen on the basis of execution, originality and aptness of interpretation.

1 Study the list of five cocktail titles below.
   a Green Angel
   b Vodkatini
   c White Roses
   d Blue Lagoon
   e Perfect Love

Jot down any ideas or associations which come to mind for each title, and what sort of design or picture you would create to express those ideas (see the example below). You may want to sketch your picture.

Example Cocktail title 'Big Splash' – swimming pool, brightly coloured sunchairs, striped umbrellas, someone diving into pool. Style – modern, 'Hollywood', poster, vivid colours, realistic drawing.

When you've finished, compare your ideas with two or three other people.

2 On your own, study the winning entries for the competition.
   1 Decide which picture goes with each of the five titles above.
   2 Give marks out of ten for each picture.
   3 Discuss your conclusions with two or three other people, and try to reach a collective decision about the order of merit – 1st prize, 2nd prize and so on.

1

2

ВОДКАТИНИ!

3

4

5

4

1 Look at the cartoon below. The artist is Posy Simmonds, whose work used to appear regularly in the *Guardian* newspaper. Discuss the following points with your partner.

1 How would you describe the 'setting' of the cartoon?

2 What exactly is Posy Simmonds making fun of, and what techniques does she use?

3 Why do you think Posy Simmonds was popular with readers of the *Guardian*?

2 In groups of three or four read the summary of the 'story' of the cartoon below. Each italicized phrase refers to an expression in the cartoon. See if you can find the original expressions.

Beazeley and Buffin's *clever, up to the minute* product is a cleaning material called 'Cleanajiffy'. Traditionally, the people they would *try to sell the product to* would be women. But today things have changed. *Men* do the housework as well as *women*. Mr Tomkin pities these new modern oppressed men, *poor things*. He thinks it's the fault of the Women's Liberation Movement, which encourages women to shake off their traditional role with symbolic gestures, such as *burning their bras*. Mr Baker is tired of hearing about women's rights, and *under no circumstances would he use* a cleaning product such as Cleanajiffy himself. However, Beazeley and Buffin have a reputation to maintain. They have always *kept up with new ideas*, and been responsive to *changes in the way people behave*. Consequently, they are trying to make their product attractive to *modern couples*, bearing in mind that *the idea modern society has* of the modern couple is very different from the one it had of the traditional couple.

5

1 ☐ David talks about his work in advertising and the audiences he writes for. How does he describe the stereotyped audience represented in the cartoon on the left?

2 Which of the characteristics listed below are attributed to 'the *Guardian* reader'? Listen again if necessary.

cultured	liberal	cynical
works in advertising	works in marketing	centrist
left of centre	fairly moderate	socially aware
socially active	committed	intellectual snob
doesn't like to be talked down to	radical	

3 What adjective was used to describe the piece of writing that David did for 'someone like himself'?

6

1 In groups of three or four quickly note down two or three cinema or TV advertisements which have made a particularly strong impression on you. Describe one of the advertisements on your list to the rest of the group, explaining why you like it or dislike it.

2 *Cosmopolitan* magazine did a survey in the UK to find the advertisements that people liked best and came up with the list below. Read through it and try to guess what the underlined expressions mean.

COSMO'S TOP TEN ADS

1 **Levis 501s**: (jeans) Two <u>great</u> TV and cinema ads using original songs—Sam Cooke's *Wonderful World*, Marvin Gaye's *Heard it Through the Grapevine*. Beautiful men in <u>evocative American settings</u>.

2 **Pimms**: (a cocktail) <u>Quick-fire succession of images</u> showing a young couple drinking Pimms through the years. <u>Fascinating catalogue of changing trends in hair and fashion</u>. You keep wishing it would slow down to give you a better look.

3 **Brylcreem**: (hair cream for men) <u>Highly atmospheric ads, with a 'Fifties feel. Shot in black and white</u> with the sole exception of the red Brylcreem jar. <u>Dated soundtrack and style, evocative</u> of old TV programmes.

4 **The *Guardian***: (a newspaper) Departure from usual <u>vox-pop or celebrity ads</u>. One ad shows that things aren't always what they seem, i.e. <u>skinhead</u> is saving the businessman rather than attacking him. The other celebrates the *Guardian*'s editorial freedom: the only paper puppet without strings.

5 **Pirelli**: (tyres) <u>Thriller storyline</u> of wife planning to kill husband by fixing brakes on his car, then preparing to meet her lover. <u>Plans thwarted by superb holding</u> of Pirelli tyres. Good use of Doors' song *Riders on the Storm*.

6 **Coke**: (Coca Cola) <u>Nice, bright, bubbly, happy scenarios depicting</u> the All-American dream. <u>Series of shots</u>—baseballing, rollerskating, clean-living young Yanks—with <u>snappy soundtrack music</u>.

7 **Holsten Pils**: (lager) <u>Clever editing of vintage black and white movie footage</u> to incorporate comedian Griff Rhys-Jones seemingly conversing with stars such as Humphrey Bogart, Peter Cushing and Edward G Robinson.

8 **Benson & Hedges**: (cigarettes) <u>Very clever, often obscure, always beautifully photographed</u> ads. Immediately recognisable, even though the <u>name is not overtly used</u>.

9 **Halifax Building Society**: (organisation that accepts deposits and lends out money to people who want to build or buy houses) Series of magazine ads showing the horrors of flat-sharing—tiny rooms crowded with <u>larger than life</u> people.

10 **British Telecom**: (the main supplier of telecommunications services in the UK) <u>BT hit on a winner</u> using <u>prattling</u> penguins.

7 Planning an advertising campaign

You work for an advertising agency, and a well-known jeans manufacturer has asked you to handle the publicity campaign for their latest product. They are planning to launch a new line in 'luxury' jeans. They are aiming at the upper end of the market, and wish to convey an image which is simultaneously sophisticated and sexy. The director of the agency has asked you to work in teams on ideas for a 30-second TV spot, and to think of a name for the jeans, before reconvening in one large group to try to choose the best idea.

Team briefing 30-second TV spot: jeans.

Points to consider:
1 Do we want a story line? If so, what? (thriller, western, romance, boy meets girl, etc.)
2 Actors? (famous – specific suggestions? unknowns? stuntpeople?)
3 Soundtrack: music? If so, what sort? (song, instrumental, pop, classic, etc.) dialogue? (script ideas) voice over? (message?) type of language used?
4 Setting (where? what period? indoor/outdoor shots?)
5 Atmosphere/ambience/mood – what sort of feel are we aiming at?
6 Photography – special effects? colour? black and white? speed? focus?

Problems There are some really good jeans advertisements already. We need to come up with a winner, but it's got to be original and memorable.

Notes to the team As your ideas begin to take shape, decide how you are going to present them to the rest of the group at the final meeting. Will there be just one spokesperson, or do you want to break your presentation into different sections, with different speakers? Do you need any of the following?
white board
OHP
tape-recorder/record player
video camera
actors

If you are going to present your ideas in the form of a talk without any visual aids, you will have to express yourself clearly and convincingly in order to give your listeners a good picture of what you have in mind – the highlighted expressions in the *Cosmopolitan* list on page 53 may be useful.

Final presentation Teams reconvene for a final meeting. After the presentations, try to reach a consensus about which spot the agency should use.

UNIT 7　THE RIGHT STUFF

1

1　🔊　Listen to the different parts of the tape and see if you can put a name to the emotion or feeling that each one suggests, e.g. anger, excitement, puzzlement, disgust, passion, alienation, etc.

2　In groups of three or four discuss what physical symptoms you experience when you're afraid. Do you, for example, go hot or cold? Does your stomach knot up? Do you go white, yellow, grey or green with fear? (All these colours are possible in English! What about in your own language?) When you've finished, try to complete together the following expressions to describe different states of fear.

I got cold _____ .
My _____ ran cold.
It made my _____ creep.
It was positively _____ raising.
I completely lost my _____ .
I was scared out of my _____ .
It was _____ chilling.

Clue: the missing words are all related to the body or organism, e.g. nerve, blood, teeth, hair, ribs, spine, collarbone, flesh, wits, toes, feet. Discuss your conclusions with the rest of the class, comparing with examples from your own language.

2

Divide into two groups, A and B. Read the text for your group carefully, making sure that you can remember the most important details of the story. You may make notes if you wish. Get together with one student from the other group and report to each other, as accurately as possible, the events related in the two texts. You may refer to your notes but not to the text itself.

With your partner from the other group, try to decide:
1　In what way the two stories are similar.
2　What the people in the stories have in common.

Compare your conclusions with the rest of the class.
Text for Group A on page 56.
Text for Group B on page 57.

Group A Text

A Lark in the Arc

Napoleon commissioned it, de Gaulle marched in its shadow—and it remains one of the crowning symbols of France. Besides, it's *there*. So on a sleepy Sunday morning last week, when photographers and television crews just happened to be on hand, Parisian pilot Alain Marchand, 46, threaded a single-engine Morane "Rallye" through Paris's Arc de Triomphe. His plane, christened Question Mark, approached the Arc at 100 miles per hour—and its 31.5 foot wingspan passed through with only eight feet to spare on either side. Marchand thus became the second pilot to pull off the stunt (a biplane did it in 1919) and gained publicity for his favourite complaint: the rising taxes and other costs discouraging amateur flight. But Marchand violated a raft of Parisian overflight laws—and now must navigate his way through the courts on a wing and a prière.

Glossary

to be on hand: to be present

to thread (something through something): to pass through a narrow opening (like thread through the eye of a needle)

to christen: to give a name to someone or something

wingspan: the distance between the tips of each wing

spare: left over, additional to what is needed

a stunt: a special feat, performance or trick, often difficult or dangerous

to pull off: to succeed in doing something difficult

a raft (US): a large collection or number

to zip through something: to do something very quickly

Group B: Text

Paris by Air
Taking an Eiffel chance

Since it was completed by Alexandre-Gustave Eiffel in 1889, Paris's 984-ft Eiffel Tower has been assaulted in just about every bizarre way thrill seekers could conceive. A Parisian baker established the tradition when the tower was scarcely three years old by wobbling non-stop up 363 steps to the first platform. On stilts. In 1923, while a band oom-pahed him on, a local sportswriter bumped all the way in the opposite direction. On a bicycle. That record was smashed 35 years later by a stuntman from Saint-Tropez who descended the stairs on a unicycle. Because it was there, squads of mountaineers have attempted to climb the iron framework Alpine-style; not until 1964 did four experienced climbers finally reach the top.

Not all the assaults, unfortunately, ended well. In 1901 a Hungarian tailor stepped off the tower in the first, and only, test of a spring-loaded, batwing flying cape he had devised; he plunged to his death.

Last week, inevitably, the first parachute jump from the top of the Eiffel Tower went into its book of absurdities. British Skydiver Mike McCarthy and his girlfriend, Amanda Tucker, first made several exploratory visits, posing as tourists. On their ultimate trip, the pair suddenly whipped steerable parachutes out of their knapsacks and worked their way through two antisuicide wire screens that surround the top level. As onlookers screamed "Don't do it!" Tucker pushed off, followed by McCarthy. In the gentle breeze of a clear spring day, they floated down and, landing in the Champs de Mars, gathered up their gear and sauntered off. Press reports cooed about the "lovers' leap", but tower officials were not amused. Said one: "It sets a very bad precedent."

Glossary

to conceive: to imagine
to wobble: to move unsteadily
stilts: poles with rests for feet, to enable people to walk at a distance above the ground
to oom-pah: (invented verb) the sound made by brass instruments in a band
a stunt (a stuntperson): a special feat, performance or trick often difficult or dangerous
a unicycle: a 'bicycle' with only one wheel
squads: large numbers
a batwing cape: a sort of coat with no sleeves, in the shape of bats' wings (Count Dracula style)
to devise: to invent
skydiver: a parachutist
to pose as: to pretend to be
to whip out: to pull (something) out quickly
gear: equipment
to saunter: to stroll, to walk in a leisurely way

3 **The Right Stuff**

1 Before you read the article, look at the photos.

Interview your partner, and make notes on his/her answers to the following questions.

1 Are you impressed by stunts like these, or do you disapprove of them? Give reasons for you answer.
2 Have you read a book by Tom Wolfe called *The Right Stuff* (or seen the film)? What do you think the expression 'the right stuff' means in relation to people like these?
3 Have you ever seen or heard of a similar stunt? Describe briefly what happened?

2 Now read the following extract from an article by David T Lykken in *Psychology Today*. After you've read it, write three or four lines summarising what the author says about 'the right stuff' and compare what other students have written.

To Shakespeare, fear was "of all base passions . . . most accurs'd." For most of us, fear is often an unwelcome, even a shameful burden; we'd be happier without it. That is why we may envy that minority of mankind—the adventurers—who seem to have conquered fear, or perhaps never had any to begin with.

Recall Chuck (now Brigadier General) Yeager, prototype of the elite fraternity of military test pilots from which the first astronauts were chosen. It was Yeager who concealed broken ribs that he had suffered in a wild midnight horseback ride, so that he could go aloft in the belly of a B-29, wedge himself into the tiny cockpit of the X-1 rocket plane, and let himself be jettisoned at 26,000 feet to become the first man to travel faster than the speed of sound.

Tom Wolfe's book *The Right Stuff* records the exploits of Yeager and the original astronauts. But the book is not about people with a death wish or about kamikaze fanatics.

The 'right stuff' is the ability to walk on the brink of the abyss and keep your footing, to fly to the edge of the unknown and keep your wits about you, to function coolly and effectively in the face of looming, screaming stress. Many people might be able to shut their eyes and ride an experimental rocket plane into near space, 20 miles up. But when the engine flames out and the plane begins to plummet like a giant bomb, it takes someone with the right stuff, someone like Yeager, to improvise manœuvres to regain control, to save the great bird if possible, but, in any case, to survive.

I think that the essence of the "stuff" of which Wolfe wrote can be found in the personality trait of fearfulness—or, as I call it, "fear IQ". People high in this trait avoid risk and stress and strong stimulation; they seek out sheltered environments and are vulnerable to some kinds of psychiatric and psychosomatic disorders. People at the low end, those endowed with a low fear IQ, are the group from which we get our adventurers, our explorers, our astronauts, often our leaders.

It is plain that society needs such people. Were it not for the fact that a small percentage of every generation has this quality of relative fearlessness, we would not have advanced this far as a species. The Wright brothers might have gotten their airplane assembled, but no one would have risked flying it. The North American continent, in fact, would never have been discovered.

Glossary

base: morally low
accursed: ill-fated, miserable
burden: something which oppresses us, weighs upon us
recall: remember
aloft: up into the sky
to wedge: push into a small, uncomfortable space
jettisoned: released
kamikaze: Japanese aircraft full of explosives deliberately crashed by its pilot: or the pilot of such a plane
brink: edge
abyss: a deep, almost bottomless gulf or chasm (often found in mountains)
keep your wits about you: remain calm, clear-headed
looming: threatening, approaching
plummet: to fall suddenly and fast
psychosomatic: caused or aggravated by mental stress
endowed with: possessing (naturally)
gotten: (American) past participle of 'got'

3 Have *you* got the right stuff? Here's an interview to try with a partner, followed by Professor Lykken's 'Fear IQ' test. But don't worry if you turn out to be a horrible coward – Professor Lykken has still got a few more things to say about fearless people – and they are not all complimentary!

Interview your partner and make notes on his/her answers ready for some statistics at the end.

1 What is the most frightening experience you can remember?
2 Think of three things that frighten you, even if you have never actually experienced them (e.g. war).
3 Did you have difficulty thinking of things that frighten you?
4 Have you ever done anything relatively dangerous, just for fun (e.g. parachute jumping, driving a car very fast, etc.)? Describe the activity, and your feelings about it.

Report back to the rest of the class. Use your interview notes to try and establish a few group statistics.

1 What percentage of the class was afraid of:
  a physically frightening things (such as very bad injuries, illnesses, etc.)?
  b psychologically/sociologically frightening things (such as racism, mob violence, etc.)?
  c paranormal things (such as ghosts, witchcraft, etc.)?
2 What percentage of the class enjoys doing relatively dangerous things? What percentage of the class *enjoyed* doing dangerous things when they were younger, but has now 'calmed down'?

Now try the 'Fear IQ' test below. Before you start, decide whether you think you are relatively fearful, average, or relatively fearless in view of what you have just been discussing with the others in your group.

YOUR FEAR IQ

The psychological test called the Activity Preference Questionnaire measures fear of real, physical dangers as well as apprehensiveness in the face of social uncertainty. From the way you respond to the following items excerpted from the test, you can get a rough idea of how fearless you are.

Imagine yourself in the two situations in each of the following pairs. Pretend that one or the other *must* happen to you, and then tick the one that you would consider the lesser evil.

1 Cleaning up your house after floodwaters have left it filled with mud.
   Making a parachute jump.
2 You spend hours fixing a fancy barbecue for some guests, but they eat very little and seem not to like it.
   Distributing 1,000 handbills in mailboxes from door to door.

3 Having to walk around all day on a blistered foot.
   Sleeping out on a camping trip in an area where rattlesnakes have been reported.
4 You're in a bank and suddenly three masked men with guns come in and make everyone raise their hands.
   Sitting through a two-hour concert of bad music.
5 You have to stay in bed all day with the flu and a sick headache.
   Some fast-talking person at a party starts teasing you unmercifully and your face begins to burn and your hands to tremble.
6 Having the pilot announce that there is engine trouble and he may have to make an emergency landing.
   Working a week in the fields digging potatoes.

7 Finding out people have been gossiping about you.
Working all day in the hot sun.

8 Being a restaurant dishwasher for one week.
Being interviewed on TV, you become tongue-tied and make a poor showing.

9 While with a group of new people you try to tell a story but the others talk and no one listens to you.
You have parked your car in a public lot and return to find a big dent in the door.

10 Being at a circus when suddenly two lions get loose down in the ring.
Arriving at the circus and discovering that you've forgotten your tickets.

11 Washing a car.
Driving a car at 95 miles an hour.

12 Asking someone to pay you money that s/he owes you.
Sleeping one night on the floor.

One alternative in each pair describes a frightening or embarrassing situation; the other chances are that you are relatively fearless. Of 1,000 people who have completed the full questionnaire, ten per cent of the men and one percent of the women chose the frightening alternative in more than three-quarters of the items. The risk-avoiders, who chose the frightening option in fewer than a quarter of the items, included three per cent of the men and eight per cent of the women.

Were you right in your self-evaluation?

4 In the article, Professer Lykken puts forward the thesis that the trait of fearlessness can also lead to 'the wrong stuff' as well as 'the right stuff' and that people who demonstrate this trait may end up as psychopaths rather than as heroes, depending on how they were brought up. He quotes studies which demonstrate that psychopaths are fearless in the face of imminent pain, such as electric shocks. He says, 'In short, my thesis is that the hero and psychopath are twigs from the same branch.' He concludes . . .

My conjecture that only one trait, fearlessness, accounts for the full syndrome of the psychopathic personality is by no means generally accepted. Any theory that contends that a Chuck Yeager might just as well have become a con man needs considerably more testing and support before most people will believe it.

Meanwhile, I shall continue to add to my collection of newspaper clippings of Medal-of-Honour winners who take to robbing banks, much-decorated police officers who are discovered to be running burglary rings, widely admired Presidents with extravagant sex lives, astronauts whose leisure-time diversions are naughty or dangerous or both. And I shall continue to believe that while we still need these relatively fearless men and women, we also need to keep a careful eye on them. Even ones who avoid psychopathy and whose boldness, aggressiveness, and charm elevate them to positions of leadership, even these can be dangerous, because, among other things, they are not sufficiently frightened of war. They are willing to risk wars or to start them, and, when they do, there are always other heroes eager to do the fighting.

Does Lykken's argument sound convincing to you? Discuss your opinions with the others in your class.

4 ***Part one*** 😐

1 Look at the following adjectives.
terrified   anxious   frightened   nervous   apprehensive   worried

With a partner, rank them from one to six, with number one representing the strongest of these emotions.

2 Look at the list of things below. Which one do you find the most frightening? Rank them from one to six, with number one representing the most frightening. Compare your answers with those of two or three other people.

snakes   heights   sharks   death   disease   financial problems

3 On the tape you will hear Annie and Tim discussing a survey which was done in the USA. Read through the questions below, and as you listen to the tape for the first time, try to answer them.

  1 In what way does Annie's list of frightening things differ from the one you looked at in question 2 above?
  2 What does Tim fear most?
  3 Why is Tim surprised?
  4 What reason does he give for his surprise?

Check your answers with a partner, putting a question mark beside any areas that are not clear. As you listen a second time:

  1 Check for any information which wasn't clear on the first listening.
  2 Listen to the way in which Tim says the following things:
    'Could you repeat those again?'
    'I'm really surprised.'
    Is there anything that strikes you about them (tone of voice, meaning, intonation, etc.)?

Part two 😐

1 Do a round-the-class survey to find out how many people:
  a have ever spoken in front of a group (give details – size, reason, etc.)
  b have never spoken in front of a group but think they would feel frightened
  c have never spoken in front of a group but think they would enjoy it

2 Annie asks Tim what advice he would give to speech anxiety sufferers. Working with a partner, list some of your own ideas in the table on page 63.
As you listen, put a tick by any of your ideas that Tim mentions. Make notes on his suggestions.

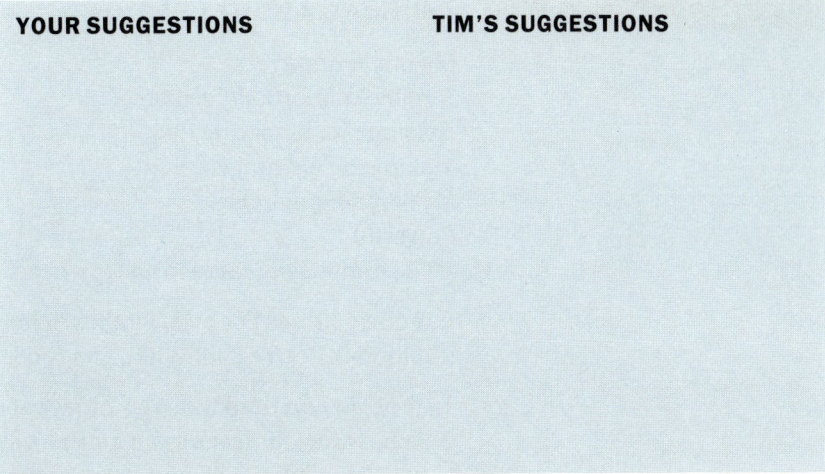

YOUR SUGGESTIONS   **TIM'S SUGGESTIONS**

3 On your own, look at Tim's suggestions, and the suggestions below made by the writer of the article that Tim and Annie have been discussing. Tick those you agree with and put a cross by those you disagree with. When you've finished, discuss your opinions with two or three others.

TIPS FOR SPEAKERS

DECIDE ON YOUR SPECIFIC OBJECTIVES FIRST. Before you think about anything else, know one or two major points you want to communicate. Then plan the best way to get them across.

PUT YOURSELF IN YOUR AUDIENCE'S PLACE. Recognize how you and most of the audience differ in attitudes, interests and familiarity with what you are talking about. Then speak to them on their terms, in their language.

DON'T MEMORIZE, DON'T READ. Except for a few carefully chosen gems—memorable phrases or examples you know will work well—be as spontaneous as possible. Don't rehearse to the point that you find yourself saying things exactly the same way each time. Use brief notes to keep yourself organized.

SPEAK TO ONE PERSON AT A TIME. Looking at and talking to individuals in the audience helps keep you natural, it feels foolish orating at one person. Speak to that person as long as it is mutually comfortable, usually up to 15 seconds.

TRY NOT TO THINK ABOUT YOUR HANDS AND FACIAL EXPRESSIONS. Instead, concentrate on what you want to get across and let your nonverbal communication take care of itself. Conscious attention to gestures leads to inhibition and awkwardness.

TAKE IT SLOW AND EASY. People in an audience have a tremendous job of information processing to do. They need your help. Slow down, pause and guide the audience through your talk by delineating major and minor points carefully. Remember that your objective is to help the audience understand what you are saying, not to present your information in record time.

SPEAK THE WAY YOU TALK. Speak as you do in casual conversation with someone you respect. Expecting perfection is unrealistic and only leads to tension. The audience is interested in your speech, not your speaking.

ASK FOR ADVICE AND CRITICISM. For most people, careful organization and a conversational style add up to a good speech. A few speakers, however, have idiosyncrasies that distract an audience. Solicit frank criticism from someone you trust, focusing on what might have prevented you from accomplishing your objectives. Usually people can correct problems themselves once they are aware of them. If you don't feel you can, take a course in public speaking or see a speech consultant.

Glossary

get them across: communicate them
gems; jewels: 'star' points
mutually: for each other
awkwardness: lack of ease
tremendous: very great
delineating: outlining
in record time: very fast
idiosyncracies: personal mannerisms

5 | **THINKING ABOUT LEARNING**

My first language
A relief, comfortable, secret
Helping me, hindering me
Making me a stranger
My second language
Powerful
Two strange languages inside my head.

Juan Berganinos Fuentes, Pimlico School.
(Children's Poetry Exhibition, London Underground, 1988)

1 Who do you think Juan is, and what experience is he writing about?
2 What are your feelings about the way you are able to express yourself in your own language, and the way you are able to express yourself in English (or any other foreign language)?
3 How do you think your first language helps you, and how does it hinder you?
4 Discuss the following comments made by language learners.

'I feel like a fool if I ask people to repeat; I prefer to pretend I understand what they're saying.'
'In (international) meetings conducted in English, the British deliberately try to make the non-English speaking members look stupid. It's difficult to keep cool and not make mistakes.'
'I think you have to like a language and identify with the people and the culture in order to speak it well.'
'I learn better if I like my teacher, and s/he likes me.'
'I don't want to express my opinions in front of the other people in my group because I don't feel comfortable with them.'
'I think to learn a language well, you have to have a sense of fun, and be prepared to act the clown a bit.'

1 Look at the following headlines in pairs. Check you understand what they mean.

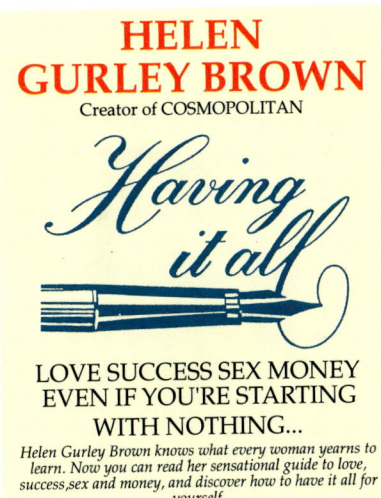

HELEN GURLEY BROWN
Creator of COSMOPOLITAN

Having it all

LOVE SUCCESS SEX MONEY
EVEN IF YOU'RE STARTING
WITH NOTHING...

Helen Gurley Brown knows what every woman yearns to learn. Now you can read her sensational guide to love, success, sex and money, and discover how to have it all for yourself.

A New English Library Paperback. On sale now.

HOW TO GET TO
THE TOP
IN A DAY

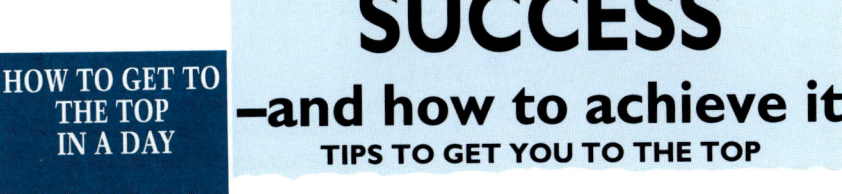

SUCCESS
–and how to achieve it
TIPS TO GET YOU TO THE TOP

If it's so tough at the top, why does
everyone want to get there?

"SUCCESS, FAME AND FORTUNE–
THEY'RE ALL ILLUSIONS.........."
Michael Jackson in *The Wiz*

Part 1

1 'Getting to the top . . .' What does this mean for you? Discuss together.
2 Tracy, Kate, Stephanie and Joanna are discussing the same question. As you listen, make notes on their answers in column A. Then try to complete Column B.

	A **Getting to the top means . . .**	**B** **Speaker's job?** **(Your speculations)**
Tracy		
Kate		
Stephanie		
Joanna		

Compare your answers with two or three other people.

Part 2 🖭

1 In your opinion do the four things mentioned by Helen Gurley-Brown – love, success, sex and money – represent 'having it all'? Compare your ideas with the rest of the class and list your suggestions on the board.

2 Below, note anything mentioned by the speakers.

Having it all ....

....

Compare this list to the one you made in class.

Part 3 🖭

1 'Courses for this, courses for that . . .' Do you think it's possible to learn how to be successful? Discuss your opinions with the rest of the class and list examples.

2 As you listen, how many of the speakers answer 'yes' to the question? What examples do they give?

Part 4 🖭

The table below shows the jobs of the speakers you heard on the tape. Were your predictions in Part One correct? The last questions they were asked were, 'Would you like to be famous?' and, 'If you could swap places with a famous person for one day, who would you choose?' Try to predict their answers before you listen. As you listen, complete the right-hand column.

	YOUR PREDICTION	THEIR ANSWER
Tracy songwriter/singer		
Kate keep fit instructor		
Stephanie nanny		
Joanna secretary		

If you could meet one of the speakers, who would you choose, and why? Discuss your choice with the rest of the class.

2 In groups of three or four, look at the following list of words. They are all related to the idea of success.
achievement, commitment, kudos, charisma, fantasy, identity, aspirations, status, inhibitions, assertiveness, self-esteem

Below are the definitions of these eleven words. Divide them between your groups, and complete the blanks with an appropriate word. Each definition relates to only *one* word in the list, but you may have to change its form, e.g. achievement – achieve – achieving, etc. When you have finished, put all the definitions together.

1 _____ means glory, or fame or status. You can acquire _____ in a variety of ways, for example by knowing famous people. You can acquire _____ by what you do, or by how you behave. Winning an important contract for your firm brings you a lot of _____ . Getting invited to a tea-party at Buckingham Palace also gets you _____ .

2 To _____ is to dream, to imagine, to invent. You may spend hours _____ what you would do if you won a million pounds – exactly what you would buy, where you would live, how you would spend your life. You may _____ about yourself or your family, inventing things – _____ – that are not strictly true. Some people have a vivid _____ life – they spend hours day-dreaming, making picture stories in their minds.

3 _____ is a special power that certain people have which makes other people pay a lot of attention to them. In extreme cases, the power seems almost magical, and permits people with _____ to influence huge numbers of people. So, you could say that Christ had _____, and Hitler had _____ . On a smaller scale, it's the person with _____ who makes a party a success, who organizes games, animates people, tells funny stories, etc., or the person in a company who inspires everyone to work hard, who gets people to do what he or she wants, who leads the team. We call such people _____ .

4 To _____ to something, or to doing something means to desire it strongly. Usually it is something 'higher' than yourself, for example you can _____ to becoming Prime Minister, or becoming an astronaut; you can _____ to having a colour TV if you only have a black and white one at present; you can _____ to moving from a poor neighbourhood to a rich one. If you are the sort of person who hopes to improve your situation, and who thinks a lot about how to achieve what you want, then you are _____, perhaps an _____ writer, or an _____ factory worker. For many people _____ are an important part of life – they are what give us hope, they are a desire to improve in some way. Sometimes, they are very precious 'dreams' that lift us out of ourselves.

5 To be _____ to something is to be very interested in it, very involved in it, and in making it work; to believe strongly in it. Albert Schweitzer is a good example of a person who was absolutely _____ to his work. You may have a strong sense of _____ to a project you believe in. You may have a sense of _____ to your parents for bringing you up, looking after you, and giving you love and affection.

67

6 To _____ something is to accomplish it, to carry it out, to get it, to reach it. 'Everyone would like to _____ some sort of recognition for the work they do.' 'The company has set a sales target, and would like to _____ it by the end of the year.' 'I've been working on my novel all morning, but I feel I haven't really _____ much.' 'What exactly do you want to _____ in life?' When we do something really satisfying, we have a sense of _____ . 'Passing my driving test was a real _____ .' 'I feel as though I've been wasting my time for the last year or so – I've no sense of _____.' Psychologists refer to people who do not realize their full potential as 'under-_____ or low-_____ .' Someone who did very well at school, then went to university, and finally ends up driving a taxi for a living would be an under- or low-_____ . Conversely, a person who came from a poor family, left school at the age of twelve, but who finally worked his or her way to a job as a manager, or owner of a small business, would be an over- or high-_____ . _____ in general is strongly associated with the idea of success.

7 To _____ with someone is to consider yourself as sharing charactertistics with them; consequently having a kind of imaginative sympathy with that person, and sometimes modelling your behaviour on him/her. 'I _____ more with my father than my mother.' 'I really loved that book because I could _____ totally with the heroine.' The act of _____ is called _____ . 'At school I had no sense of _____ with any of my teachers. They all seemed too old-fashioned.' We can also talk about a person's _____ – his individuality, his or her particular personality. If you have a strong sense of your _____ you know what sort of person you are; if you experience an _____ crisis, you may have problems deciding what you want in life, or what sort of person you really are.

8 To _____ means to prevent or restrain. People often feel _____ if they have to speak in front of large numbers of people. Psychologists often talk about people's _____ . These are mechanisms which prevent us from expressing what we feel in a direct way. We may refer to people as _____ or, conversely _____ . Someone who is the latter does not worry about saying what he or she feels, or doing what he or she wants. Young children are often _____ . You may have _____ about speaking in class because you're worried about making mistakes, or because you think other people will laugh at your accent.

9 _____ is position, importance, in relation to others. We often talk about someone's _____ in society. A judge, or a member of parliament, has high _____; a person who sweeps the streets does not have much social _____ . We also talk about _____ symbols, such as a Rolls Royce, a Cartier watch, an Yves St. Laurent dress, or a villa in Cannes. These are exterior signs of our _____ in society.

10 _____ is having enough self-awareness and self-confidence to know what you are worth and to insist that others recognise your rights. By learning to _____ yourself, you can negotiate situations which previously you were too shy or too insecure to handle – making sure

that your boss appreciates your work, for example, or standing up for yourself in a relationship where you feel you are being unjustly exploited.

11 _____ or a sense of self-worth, is a necessary pre-requisite for the characteristic described in the previous definition. It means thinking positively about your value as an individual. To have low _____ means you don't have a very high opinion of yourself.

3

1 📺 The four people who were interviewed in the preceding listening exercises were all in their twenties. Do you think the idea of success changes as we get older? If so, in what way? List your ideas on the board.

Kaye (in her forties) and Lawrence (seventy) were asked to comment on the notion of success. Answer the questions below as you listen to what they say.

1 Kaye's reaction to the quotation 'having it all . . . love, success, sex and money' is one of:
amusement ☐
surprise ☐
interest ☐

2 Kaye's idea of 'having it all' is:
basically the same as the previous speakers' ☐
different from the previous speakers' ☐

3 Kaye feels that happiness is linked to the idea of:
self-acceptance ☐
self-questioning ☐

4 Lawrence feels the previous speakers:
expressed themselves inarticulately ☐
had too much to say ☐
expressed themselves well ☐

5 Lawrence puts the priority on:
health ☐
wealth ☐

6 Commenting on the views of the previous speakers, Lawrence:
finds them faulty ☐
finds them entertaining ☐
sympathizes with them ☐

2 😑 **A cat's eye view of success**

As you listen look at the cartoon below. How accurately do the pictures represent the details of the story? Make notes on any differences.

4

1 Look at the following headlines. What do they mean? What are your reactions?

THEY SAY SHE WEARS $4 MILLION-WORTH OF JEWELS TO LUNCH

SOAP SPRINGS ETERNAL

THE FACE OF WEALTH

The extravagant lifestyle of Candy Spelling upstages even that of soap opera heroine Krystle Carrington.

2 Soap operas have had a huge success in the last couple of decades. In Britain, for example, 35 million people watched the episode of *Dallas* in which the hero-villain JR got shot.

1 Name as many popular British, American and Australian soap operas as you can think of.
2 Which of the programmes pictured below are shown on TV in your own country?

3 If you can, give examples of any soap operas produced by TV or film companies in your country. Are they basically the same as the 'American model' or do they have strong cultural differences?

3 Choose one of the following simulations. Simulation 1 (page 72) is about what makes a successful soap opera; Simulation 2 (page 77) is about what makes a successful magazine.

SIMULATION 1

Choosing the Right Soap

You are a member of the Production Team at IBT, a large American TV network. Your viewing figures have been falling dramatically while the nation switches to rival channels to watch series like *Dallas* and *Dynasty*. IBT is now in serious financial difficulty, and the future of the channel is at stake. One of the things you need to help get the ailing network back on its feet is a new 'soap'. Your research team has made a short list of three possible ideas for the new series, but so far nothing has been decided.

1 Split into three groups A, B, C. Group A read synopsis 1 (below), Group B synopsis 2 (page 74), Group C synopsis 3 (page 75). Make notes on your reactions.

2 Reconvene in small working groups of three people (one from Group A, one from Group B, one from Group C).

3 Work through the following points.

   a Brainstorming session to decide on the key ingredients for a successful series.

   b Individual reports on the three synopses.

   c Decisions: which series, if any, sounds like a potential winner? Are there changes/alterations that need to be made? What about possible endings?

   d Provisional casting list: which stars might fit which roles?

   e Planning an alternative series: if you don't like any of the three ideas, try to come up with other suggestions.

After you've finished, reconvene with the whole Production Team and try to reach a final decision about which of the series to launch, or alternatively, the next steps to be taken if all three are rejected.

Plot synopsis 1: A Romance

Title?

Setting: America in the twenties and thirties.

Julietta Rafael, beautiful, spoiled daughter of millionaire businessman with Mafia connections, lives a life of thoughtless luxury. Caught up in the wild fever that hit western society after the end of the First World War, Julietta's life is a constant round of parties and balls, set against the music of the period – jazz, the Charleston, etc. At one of these parties, Julietta meets a handsome young man whose dreamy, delicate air at first intrigues, then fascinates her. Henry Barnet, the only son of an aristocratic U.S. Senator, is socially far above Julietta; besides, he is engaged to be married to the girl next door (also rich and also aristocratic). This does not prevent Julietta falling madly in love with him. Used to having her own way, she determines to make him love her in return. Henry, who is basically weak, tries feebly to resist, but the struggle is unequal. At a weekend houseparty, the two become lovers. Henry, overcome with guilt and remorse, tries to break free, without success. Finally he agrees to elope with Julietta; but on the eve of their departure, he loses his nerve, breaks down and confesses to his father.

The incident provokes a terrible scene; scandal breaks over the two households, and Julietta's father, in a fury, sends her off to a finishing school in Switzerland. Julietta is heartbroken at Henry's weakness; she hates her school, and finally, after various scenes of rebellion, runs away to Paris. It is there that news breaks of the Wall Street Crash. Julietta, opening the newspaper one day, comes face to face with the news of her father's suicide. Returning to America she finds herself a penniless orphan. She is forced to grow up and face reality. At her wits end for a solution to her problems, she approaches Marcello Platini, one of her father's connections, and asks him for a job. Times are hard and Platini is a busy man – he tells her there is nothing except work as a waitress in one of his restaurants. Julietta accepts. Platini, expecting her to give up after the first week, is surprised by her courage and determination. Her new life is hard. Besides the long hours, she must also face the hostility of her workmates, and the constant problem of making ends meet. Platini, who comes to the restaurant often, begins to take an interest in her; the staff too, are finally won over by her courage.

Julietta's beauty wins her many admirers, but she can't forget Henry, in spite of his behaviour, and shows no interest in other men. One evening a group of people enter. Julietta, approaching to take their order, comes face to face with Henry. She makes an involuntary move towards him; he turns pale, ignores her, and hurries his friends out of the restaurant. Julietta is stunned and mortified. She loses all hope; returning to her miserable room after work, she cuts her wrists.

Platini, a witness to the scene in the restaurant, follows her, and discovers what has happened. In the hospital, Julietta tells him that she hates him for saving her life. Implacable, Platini refuses to show any sympathy, and tells her that a new job awaits her. He is making her assistant to the Manager of a new hotel due to open the following month. He will expect her to be ready to start her training in a week's time. Julietta's pride is stung; she rises to Platini's challenge and forces herself back into the world. Believing that she will never love another man, she throws herself passionately into her work. Platini watches her steady progress, and realizes that he is falling in love with her.

Julietta is still surrounded by admirers, all of whom she ignores. One of these is a powerful Mafia boss called Aldo Pezzi. Seeing his advances frustrated, Pezzi arrives at the hotel one evening in an ugly mood; he forces himself into Julietta's room. A struggle ensues; the staff, alerted by Julietta's screams, call Platini, who arrives in a fury and beats up Pezzi, flinging him out into the street. This episode starts a gang vendetta; Platini, leaving his house one day is gunned down by Pezzi's men. The news is brought to Julietta – frantic with fear, she rushes to the hospital, where Platini hangs between life and death. Suddenly, Julietta realizes she is in love with him. At his bedside, she pours out her feelings and begs him not to die . . .

Note: Should Platini die? Should Henry be brought in again? What about introducing a baby somewhere?

Could we get some 'big' older generation film stars, e.g. Brando, De Niro? (Budget??!)

Plot synopsis 2: The Supernatural

Title: The Quest(?)

Setting: Present day America.

Jack and Sarah Collins are twins. In early childhood their parents become aware of strange affinities existing between the two children – each seems to know, without words, how the other is feeling, and what the other is thinking. This 'telepathy' exists even when they are apart. Sarah, on a picnic with some friends, gets lost in the woods. Jack is able to locate her, telling his parents that he can 'see' her sitting by the side of a river, near a waterfall. Later, Jack falls and breaks a leg when on a climbing expedition with his school. Sarah, at home, turns pale and faints. On regaining consciousness, she tells her mother of the accident, later confirmed by a phone call from the school. The two children spend almost all their free time together. Later, as they grow up, the inevitable separation arrives, when each goes off to college, Sarah to New Hampshire, Jack to Connecticut. The two maintain contact however, writing and phoning regularly, particularly if either 'feels' the other has a problem. Then one day tragedy strikes.

Sarah, returning to her room one winter evening after a dance class, disappears. A witness claims to have seen her attacked by two men and thrown into a car, but can give no details beyond the fact that the car was a dark colour. The Collins family, frantic with worry, wait while the police hunt for the missing girl. Jack is inconsolable; he abandons his studies and returns home, spending hours pacing up and down Sarah's old room, prey to a series of hallucinations in which he sees Sarah being attacked, Sarah in a car driving through miles of corn fields, Sarah in a small café with an old-fashioned juke box. At other times, he sees her in the middle of a crowd of people; he hears chanting, and smells incense. He pesters the police constantly, telling them of his conviction that Sarah has been kidnapped, that she has been taken out of the State, that she is still alive. The police, in exasperation, finally ignore him and spend less and less time on a search which they believe is fruitless. Even Jack's parents finally resign themselves to the idea that their daughter is dead. His mother sinks into a depression; his father immerses himself in his work.

Jack is obsessed by the idea his twin is still alive. He can see her face, swollen and puffy, he can hear her calling to him. Finally, almost crazy, he gives up the idea of returning to college and sets off on a quest for his sister that will lead him across the United States, working his way doing odd jobs, keeping his eyes and ears open for signs that his sister may have passed this way. At last he picks up a clue; this leads him further west, following odd scraps of information that convince him he is finally on the right track. His search brings him to California, where, driven by his visions, and his conviction that his sister is still trying to contact him, he finds himself at last face to face with the high stone walls and the barred gate of a private estate. Behind these walls, is the sinister Dr Mishi, and the hundreds of followers who constitute his sect. Jack is sure that his sister is there, among their number. But will he ever be able to reach her, faced with the formidable security precautions that surround the sect, and the fanatical character of Dr Mishi himself? And if he ever succeeds in penetrating the closed ranks of the sect, will his sister recognise him after all this time? Will she want to leave with him? And will he be able to help her if she does?

Note: Should Jack get inside? Should he see Sarah in the street, in some kind of demo? Should they have a 'telepathic' meeting? Should this be scary/horror or more like science fiction? Special effects?

Plot synopsis 3: A Thriller

Title?

Setting: Present day Spain and Europe.

The police of several countries are beginning to be seriously worried about increasing drug traffic between the Middle East and Europe. Their research shows that one man seems to control the biggest international drug-ring in existence – one man, about whom the police know nothing, except that he is a mastermind of an organisation, a cold and clever operator on a grand scale. His code name: Nemo.

While Interpol set traps and pursue fruitless trails, Nemo plans his greatest operation yet. One day, in the Madrid office of Spanish shipping magnate, Don Ramon Martinez Catala, the telephone rings. Martinez hears the terrified voice of his daughter Cristina sobbing out words which freeze his blood. Cristina is being held by kidnappers at gunpoint. If Martinez wishes to see his daughter alive, he must do exactly as he is told. Horrified, he can only listen helplessly while a cold voice spells out his instructions. Martinez puts down the phone in a daze. The instructions were short and precise. He must immediately set in motion steps for a merger between his company and that of the owner of the world's largest fleet of tankers, Greek mutimillionaire, Socrates Atalides, a larger than life figure whose marriages, divorces, adventures and breath-taking business deals make the headlines in the world's press.

Martinez, fearing for his daughter's life, can only do what he is told. He begins proceedings for the merger. The news breaks in the press and the business world is rocked to its foundations. Martinez is beseiged by reporters. Outwardly calm, he deals with the publicity and the violent reactions of the other shareholders through a mixture of bluff and autocracy. Alone, he realizes the desperateness of the situation, and faces the chilling thought that the kidnappers will not keep their side of the bargain. Finally, at his wits end, he telephones an old friend, the only person who may be able to help him.

Adam Grace is the darling of the international jet set – handsome, blond, dashing, the heir to a considerable fortune. Only one or two of his closest friends suspect the existence of another man behind the public mask. For Grace is none other than the Fox, formerly of MI5, now freelance buccaneer and troubleshooter for intelligence services throughout the world. Grace immediately agrees to help his old friend, and sets out on a man-hunt that will take him to Greece, the Middle East and finally to Spain, to coincide with the arrival of Atalides in person to sign the famous merger. Atalides has arrived on his legendary yacht, bringing with him a much-publicized gift, made by eastern craftsmen, to commemorate the union of the two giant shipping companies. This gift, the subject of much speculation and rumour, will be presented to Martinez at a fabulous banquet on board the yacht. Its exact nature remains shrouded in mystery.

Grace, arriving at Algeciras on the evening of the banquet, observes the glittering spectacle of the port, crammed with Rolls Royces depositing the famous arrivals at the crimson carpeted area in front of Atalides' yacht. Time is running out. Pushing his way through agitated crowds of police and pressmen with popping flashbulbs, Grace reaches his parked Ferrari and roars off out of the city along the road leading to Granada, and thence to Madrid: the road along which, later that evening, will pass the armoured convoy bearing the legendary gift to the head offices of Martinez Shipping in Madrid.

On board the yacht, the sumptuous banquet draws to a close, the speeches are over, and the moment of the presentation has arrived. The lights dim and all eyes turn to the podium at the end of the vast dining room. There is a roll of drums the velvet curtains swish back, and revealed in the beam of a powerful spotlight is Atalides' fabulous gift. It is an immense statue of the famous Trojan horse of legend, made of beaten gold. A gasp goes up in the room, applause breaks out, and Martinez accepts the gift from his new business partner.

Under the careful surveillance of the police, the statue is loaded into the armoured vehicle and sets out on the journey through the mountains to Madrid. And so Atalides, under the very noses of the police, succeeds in smuggling a record-breaking quantity of heroin from the Middle East into Spanish territory. For the belly of the horse contains the evil white powder which had made Atalides the most wanted man in Europe, Nemo. In the cold wind that whistles across the jagged peaks of the Sierra Nevada, Nemo's men lie in ambush, waiting for the armoured car and its priceless booty. But while Nemo laughs at the stupidity of the police, and lifts the telephone to give the final orders to Cristina's kidnappers, the Fox puts into action his desperate and dangerous plan to save Martinez's daughter, foil the ambushers of the Golden Horse, and bring to justice the mad Greek.

Note: Should Grace die at the end? Should he marry Cristina? Should this be a James Bond style comedy/thriller, or something more serious? Should we add more to Grace's character – supernatural powers like Superman? What about the success of an Indiana Jones figure in the Spielberg series (*Raiders of the Lost Ark*, etc.)? Should he have a sidekick – male? female?

SIMULATION 2

Press Success

The problem

Universe, the popular weekly magazine, is going through a difficult period. Sales figures have been dropping steadily for the past three months, and the magazine badly needs a few highly successful issues to retrieve the situation. The editor has:

1 asked the Market Research team to come up with some figures on what sort of articles are most successful in boosting sales.
2 asked the Editorial team to consider a list of topics and draw up a short list of four potential 'bestsellers'.

Action

Divide into groups of three or four. One student from each group is the Market Research expert. He or she will join the experts from the other groups, to form the Market Research team. The remaining two or three students are part of the Editorial team.

Instructions: Editorial Team

1 Look at the editor's list of eight topics for future issues.
2 Discuss which ones you think are potential bestsellers, giving reasons.
3 Draw up a short-list of the top four.
4 Meet with your representative from the Market Research team to compare findings.

EDITOR'S SUGGESTED TOPICS	
Sport	Stars/Celebrities
Health	Politics
Crime	Sex
Money	Human interest stories

Instructions: Market Research Team

1 Study the facts and figure sheet on page 78.
2 Draw up a list of the four best-selling topics, with statistics.
3 Set out your findings clearly, ready for an oral summary. Use whatever visual aids you think are necessary (whiteboard, OHP, etc.).
4 Return to your original group and present your findings clearly and concisely.

Final action

On the basis of this last meeting, plan four issues of *Universe* (cover and cover story). Finally, meet with other Editorial teams to compare your results.

MARKET RESEARCH TEAM: FACTS AND FIGURES

The French newspaper *Le Canard Enchainé* did a survey on what made magazines sell. They compared the sales figures for six French magazines: *L'Express, Le Nouvel Observateur, Paris-Match, Le Point, L'Evénemenet du Jeudi* and *VSD*. Here are extracts from their findings.

– In one year, both *L'Express* and *Le Point* devoted one out of every eight issues to the topic of HEALTH.
– In one year, twelve cover stories were devoted to one big French star, Alain Delon, and his son; thirteen were devoted to the royal family of Monaco; Princess Diana and family were also bestsellers on the CELEBRITIES front.
– In one year, *VSD* had four cover stories devoted to SEX, *Paris-Match* had two, all the others had one, except *Le Point* (none).
– In one year, ten cover stories on the topic of MONEY pushed sales figures up to new heights for *Le Nouvel Observateur, L'Express* and *Le Point*.

Extracts from circulation figures:

MAGAZINE	DATE OF ISSUE	INCREASE IN SALES
COVER STORY: CELEBRITIES		
Paris-Match	November 84	+22%
L'Express	?	+31%
L'Express	April 85	+42%
Le Point	January 85	+35%
COVER STORY: HEALTH		
Paris-Match	April 85	+42%
Le Point	January 85	+35%
COVER STORY: MONEY		
Nouvel Observateur	November 84	+113%
Nouvel Observateur	(follow up issue)	+88%
L'Express	January 85	+68%
L'Express	March 85	+68%
Le Point	January 85	+40%
COVER STORY: SEX		
Nouvel Observateur	June 85	+49%
VSD	January 85	+38%
Paris-Match	September 84	+10%

Topics that were out of favour (apart from one or two exceptions): politics, human interest stories.

Points For Discussion

1 Does a quick look at these figures suggest any conclusions?
2 Perhaps these figures are now too out of date? What are the cataclysmic events that have occurred since this report which might affect readers' interest in these topics? Or do you think that certain topics have always been, and will always be, popular with the reading public?
3 Perhaps the above statistics reflect only French attitudes. Will readers of *Universe* be interested in the same things? After all *Universe* is a magazine for English speakers which is sold worldwide, and which prides itself on being 'universal'.

After discussing these points, look at the conclusions of *Le Canard Enchaîné*: 'In the hit parade of topics, MONEY definitely came first (how to earn it, how to invest it, the tax system, etc.). Second on the list was SEX – but high class, not vulgar. A questionnaire oriented towards finding out your sexuality (with 'psychological trimmings') was a particularly big success. Third came HEALTH (diet, the medical profession, stress, modern illnesses). Number four, CELEBRITIES, seemed to be a perennial favourite.'

UNIT 2 **TESTING A TEST**

Divide into two groups.
Group A Instructions

1 Check you know the meaning of the following words and expressions.

finding	forgetful	a casual glance	a flute
an adage	lively	eye contact	an emergency
a doer	gambling	a brand of toothpaste	to lose your temper
casually	to feel upset	a practical joke	to look ahead

2 Complete the following questionnaire individually. Don't worry too much about how exact your answers are. You are trying to get a general impression.

> Answer the following questions quickly, yes or no. Write down your answers, Y for yes and N for no.
>
> 1 Do you often wish for more excitement in your life?
> 2 Are you often late for appointments?
> 3 Are you impatient with fact-finding by others when you have made up your mind about something?
> 4 Do you prefer phoning to writing letters?
> 5 Do you often say things without thinking?
> 6 Are you generous with money?
> 7 Are you impatient with detailed directions when you think you see the point?
> 8 Do you accept the adage, 'He who hesitates is lost'?
> 9 Are you an organizer, a doer or an activist?
> 10 Do you get excited when you watch competitive sports?
> 11 Are you willing to 'have a go' even when you have no experience of the task?
> 12 Do you like to go out a lot?
> 13 Do you remember the faces of people you have met casually?
> 14 Do you consider that you control your own destiny?
> 15 Are you always in a hurry?
> 16 Do you often get ideas for new projects you want to undertake?
> 17 Are you forgetful?
> 18 Do other people think you are lively?
> 19 Can you get ready to go out within half an hour after receiving an unexpected invitation?
> 20 Do you like to have other people around?
> 21 Do you enjoy gambling?
> 22 Are you able to accept changes in plans without feeling upset?
> 23 Do you prefer dogs to cats?
> 24 Will you exchange casual glances with strangers rather than avoiding eye contact?
> 25 Are you willing to try out new brands of cosmetics or toothpaste?
> 26 Do you enjoy playing games at parties?
> 27 Do you usually feel well?
> 28 Do you like to meet people?
> 29 Do you like practical jokes?
> 30 Are you inclined to enjoy the drinks tonight without worrying about tomorrow?
> 31 Would you prefer to play drums rather than a flute?
> 32 Do your friends accuse you of never relaxing?
> 33 Are you good in an emergency?
> 34 Do you lose your temper easily?
> 35 Are you always ready to look ahead even when you have real personal problems?

from Brain Games by Richard B Fisher (Fontana)

When you've finished, count up how many 'yes' answers you got, and how many 'no' answers. You'll find out how to interpret your score later. Which personality type do you think the questionnaire is trying to measure? (Check back to Unit 1).

Find a partner from Group B and turn to page 82 for further instructions.

Group B Instructions

Figure 1 (page 15) showed the seven traits which could be grouped together under the heading 'Extroversion'.

1   In the table below, read the descriptions of the seven traits.

THE EXTROVERT	THE INTROVERT
1. ACTIVITY	
. . . is physically active; is energetic and likes life to have a quick pace; has a lot of different interests	. . . gets tired easily; likes life to have a leisurely, relaxed pace; is not physically very active or energetic
2. SOCIABILITY	
. . . likes to be with other people; enjoys parties, dances and other social functions where s/he can meet and talk to people	. . . prefers the company of a few special friends; feels uncomfortable talking to people s/he doesn't know; enjoys doing things on his/her own (e.g. reading, etc.)
3. RISK-TAKING	
. . . often enjoys gambling; likes the element of 'risk' in life; likes doing things that others may consider 'dangerous'	. . . prefers to sacrifice the idea of an exciting life to a life that is familiar, safe and secure
4. IMPULSIVENESS	
. . . tends to act on the spur of the moment, to decide things impulsively; often changes his/her mind; behaves in an unpredictable way	. . . plans things in a systematic, careful way; thinks before s/he speaks or acts; 'looks before s/he leaps'
5. EXPRESSIVENESS	
. . . is inclined to show his/her emotions in public, tends to be volatile, demonstrative, sentimental, sympathetic	. . . prefers 'stiff upper lip' attitude; can be reserved, detached and generally controlled in his/her behaviour; generally even-tempered
6. REFLECTIVENESS	
. . . prefers action to theorising; is practical; enjoys doing things rather than thinking about them	. . . is interested in the abstract, the philosophical, the conceptual; enjoys knowledge for its own sake; prefers to 'think' rather than to 'do'
7. RESPONSIBILITY	
. . . is not very reliable; often late, unpredictable; sometimes irresponsible; doesn't always take his/her commitments seriously	. . . is reliable, dependable; can be trusted to fulfil commitments; serious-minded, sometimes a bit compulsive

2 Working in two sub-groups, B1 and B2, and using the descriptions to help you, design a short questionnaire which might give you some idea of whether a person has more tendencies to introversion or more tendencies to extroversion. Group B1, work on questions for traits 1, 2, 3 and 4; Group B2, work on questions for traits 5, 6 and 7. Here are some examples to give you an idea.

Question for trait 1: What sort of holiday would you prefer, a relaxing few days lying on the beach doing nothing, or an activity holiday with lots of things to do?

Question for trait 5: When you're watching a good film on TV, do you often get carried away by your emotions (e.g. laugh, cry, make comments like, 'Come on!' etc.)?

When you've finished, put all your questions together. With your complete 'questionnaire', find a partner from Group A, and do the activity below.

Groups A and B Instructions

Testing the test

1 Student B
Try out your questionnaire on your partner from Group A. Don't tell him/her what you're trying to find out.

Student A
Answer Student B's questions. Then show him/her the questionnaire you did on page 80.

2 Student B
Explain to your partner what your questionnaire was trying to measure. Show him/her the descriptions of the personality traits on page 81.

Student A
Check your score for the first questionnaire you did. Are the results of the two questionnaires similar? In your opinion, are they reasonably accurate, or 'rubbish'?

How to interpret your score for the questionnaire on page 80

If you have more 'yes' answers than 'no' answers, then you are more extroverted than introverted, and vice versa. The greater the difference between 'yes' and 'no' answers, the more you are introverted or extroverted. Remember, traits are measured on a continuum, and that it is not 'better' to be an extrovert than an introvert, nor vice versa.

UNIT 2

THE THREE-BOTTLE PROBLEM

In groups of three or four, consider the following problem. You will need: three bottles (of the same height/type), four knives (of the same type), a paper cup, some water (optional).

1   Place the three bottles upright on a table or on the floor. Position them so that each bottle forms the corner point of a triangle of equal sides. The distance between the bases of any two bottles should be slightly more than the length of a knife.

2   You now have the knives with which to construct a platform on top of the bottles. No part of any knife may touch the ground. The platform must be strong enough to support a full glass of water.

That is the problem. You may approach it as you wish. You may attack it with logic, or you may play around with the knives until something turns up. You may wait for the solution to occur to you, or you may deliberately search for it. You may even decide that the problem has no solution.

As you work on the problem observe the ease with which you solve it. Observe how long it takes you. Observe how you set about it. Observe the different approaches that you use and consider why you use them. Observe how a particular approach is blocked or comes to an end. Observe how many solutions there are, or if, in fact, there are any. If there are no solutions, observe how long it takes you to realize this and how sure you are about your decision.

The problem is intended to be an opportunity to think about your thinking. There is no frantic demand for a solution.

If you are still unsuccessful at the end of the day, you may choose to sleep on the problem, or you may choose to find out whether there is a solution by reading the next section on page 87.

When you have worked on the problem for a while, report back to the rest of the class. Has anyone found a solution? If not, turn to page 87.

UNIT 5

SIMULATION

Dressing for Work

The situation
The Linguacom School of Languages is a small school offering a variety of courses for a variety of students, but which has built up a particular reputation for specialist, short term courses aimed at the high-level business executive. In order to meet the growing demand in this area, the school recently hired two new teachers with excellent academic qualifications, James Mather and Sarah Fielding. However, a problem has arisen. Before leaving the school, students are given an 'evaluation sheet', on which, among other things, they are asked to comment on the teaching. During the last month, a number of students in James and Sarah's classes have

mentioned that, while they found the teaching itself to be satisfactory, they objected to the way the teacher was dressed (specific comments: 'teachers should not dress like hippies'; 'I object to paying a lot of money to go on a course where the teachers look as though they can't afford decent clothes'; 'clothing standards just not good enough'; 'if this is supposed to be a professional school, teachers should dress like professionals and not like students'; 'I did not pay a lot of money to spend two weeks looking at a badge saying "Don't blame me – I voted Labour"'). As staff-management relations at the school have always been informal and relaxed, the Director, Mark Harrison, decided to have a word in private with James and Sarah, in the expectation of resolving the situation amicably. To his surprise, they not only flatly refused to modify their style of dress, but accused him of being hypocritical and authoritarian. Harrison decided to let the matter drop for a while, but since then, the school has been buzzing with rumours, and there's a general feeling of grumpiness and unrest. In an attempt to get back to the good working atmosphere that previously existed, Harrison has decided to call a staff meeting to try to resolve the problem through discussion and consensus.

Before the meeting

You are a teacher at the school. Before attending the meeting, Harrison has asked you and the other members of staff to think about the specific points he has listed for discussion.

1 On your own, read through the discussion points and briefly note your reactions/opinions.
2 Add any other points that you think are relevant.

Points for discussion

1 Should the school have a (written?) policy regarding staff clothing?
2 Should the school have a policy regarding staff clothing which is applicable only to teachers teaching 'executive' courses?
3 If some sort of policy were agreed on, should the following clothing items be banned?
   jeans (too 'unprofessional')
   T shirts (same reason)
   trainers (too casual)
4 What about badges? Which of the following kinds of badges should be allowed?
   political
   religious
   human rights, e.g. Amnesty International, Gay Liberation, etc.
   joke badges
   other
5 Teachers should be free to wear what they want, but certain standards of cleanliness and tidiness should be observed (e.g. well-cut hair, clean nails, etc.)
6 There should be no clothing restrictions for staff. Instead, students should be told in the Director's pep talk at the beginning of the course that the school's philosophy of informality (students and teachers use first names,

students and teachers wear whatever they like) is based on sound pedagogical principles. (If so, which ones?)

7 We are first and foremost a business. The customer is always right.

8 We are first and foremost an educational institution. The customer may have to be willing to modify his or her views.

9 Other?

The meeting

Finally, Harrison has decided that it might be better if he, James and Sarah did not attend the first part of the meeting, but joined in later when all those not directly involved had had a chance to air their views.

Instructions

1 Elect members of staff to act as a) chairperson b) secretary.

2 Discuss the points on Harrison's list and try to reach an agreement.

3 Discuss any other points raised.

UNIT 5 CHOOSING A PARTY OUTFIT

PARTY TIME!

Jo and Chris invite you to a ... Midsummer Night's Party!! Have you always wanted to play Tarzan?? Do you secretly long to be Cleopatra?? Now is your chance!! Fancy dress only, Saturday 21st June, any time after 9pm.

Rules of the game. One person writes the names of all students on pieces of paper, twice. He or she then mixes them up, and distributes them randomly so that each student gets two names. Each person must now choose a party outfit for the two people whose names he or she has been given. Think very carefully about the choice – the outfit must suit the personality of the student. Write a description (brief) of the outfit on a piece of paper, describing the colour, the material, and any accessories (e.g. a fan, a hat, etc.).

Someone then collects the descriptions without the names of the students they are intended for, and reads them out to the class one by one. The class must try to guess which outfit is for which person. 'The designer' of the outfit must be prepared to give his or her reasons for choosing it. When all the descriptions have been read out, see how many people, if any, were given the same outfit by their two different designers.

SOLUTIONS

FROM UNIT 1

Exercise 5.3

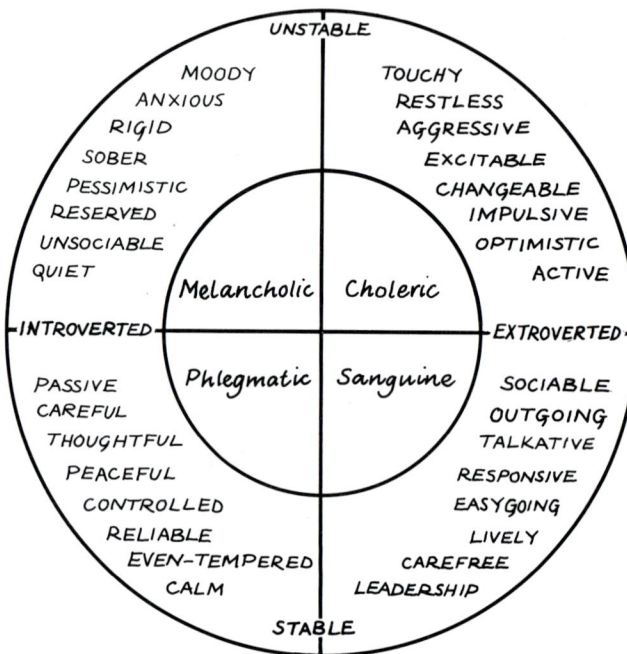

[Figure A]

FROM UNIT 2

Exercise 2.1
Test 1: 25, Test 2: 1, e; 2, c; 3, e; 4, b; 5, a

Exercise 3.1
1st quotation: Albert Einstein, 2nd quotation: Charles Darwin

Exercise 3.6

Answers to Quibble's Glasses and Steak Strategy

Prof. Quibble: It's simple. Just pick up the second glass and pour its contents into the seventh. And then pick up the fourth and pour into the ninth.

To explain Betsy's solution, call the steaks A, B, and C; each steak having sides one and two. In the first 10 minutes sides A1 and B1 are grilled. Steak B is now put aside. And in the next 10 minutes sides A2 and C1 are grilled. Steak A is now finished.

Ten more minutes and sides B2 and C2 are grilled. All three steaks cooked in only 30 minutes, right?

FROM UNIT 4
Exercise 2.2

Dane – serious; Belgian – funny; German – disciplined;
Luxemburger – discreet; Greek – hospitable; Englishman – elegant;
Frenchman – gallant; Dutchman – calm; Irishman – prolific; Italian – virile

FROM UNIT 5

Exercise 4.1

Back to Back game

When the two students re-enter the room ask them to stand back to back. Then ask each student to describe as minutely as possible what the other is wearing, without turning to look. The student who is being described may help by giving feedback or clues such as, 'Yes, that's right,' or 'Well, it's not really blue' or 'They are the sort of shoes you might wear for playing sport'.

FROM UNIT 6

Exercise 1

Picture 1: British Rail
Picture 2: Charles of the Ritz cosmetics
Picture 3: The Halifax Building Society
Picture 4: Hush Puppy Shoes. The bassett hound has always featured in their advertisements.

FROM OPTIONAL ACTIVITIES

Solution to the Three-Bottle Problem

Once it has been demonstrated, the solution is so obvious that it may seem incredible that it should have required any effort or time.

First, discard one knife completely. Because no more than four knives could be used does not mean that *all* four were required or had to be used. It is a common mistake in everyday thinking to assume that things must be done in a certain way and then to proceed from that assumption. Excellent thinking is of no use if based on an incorrect assumption. Most conjuring tricks and stage magic depends on the eagerness of the audience to take things for granted and only to start questioning things too late, when the trick has already been done.

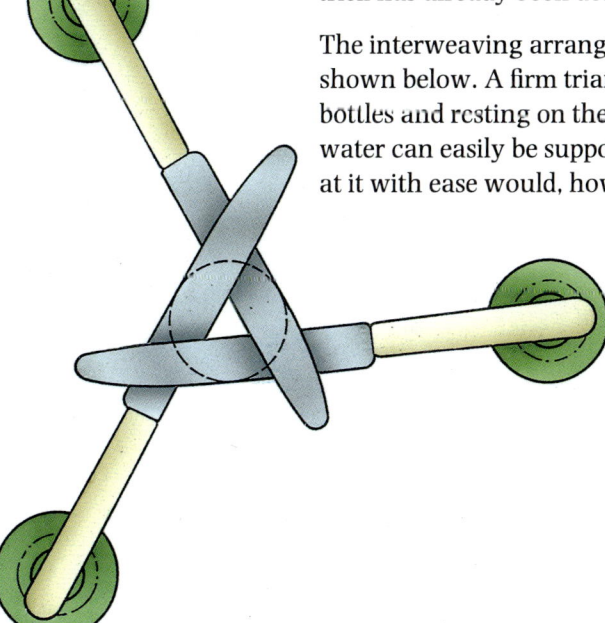

The interweaving arrangement of the knife blades to give the solution is shown below. A firm triangular-shaped platform is created between the bottles and resting on their tops. In the middle of this platform a full glass of water can easily be supported. The solution seems simple enough. To arrive at it with ease would, however, be exceptional.

Notes